R.E.I. Editions

All our ebooks can be read on the following devices:
* Computer
* eReader
* iOS
* Android
* Blackberry
* Window
* Tablet
* Mobile

Brown Kittel

Boeing B-17

The Flying Fortress

ISBN: 9782372975445

Publication: march 2025
Copyright © 2025 R.E.I. Editions
www.rei-editions.com

**Brown Kittel

3

Boeing B-17
The Flying Fortress

R.E.I. Editions

Index

B-17 Flying Fortress 9

History 10

Use 16

Operation Pointblank 29

Norden targeting system 31

The Sperry Spherical Turret 34

Technique 36

Wright R-1820 Engine 45

Versions 49

Model 299 51

Y1B-17 54

Y1B-17A 57

B-17B 59

B-17C 60

B-17D 62

B-17E 63

B-17F 66

B-17G 68

YB-40 71

PB-1 72

JB-17 73

BQ-7 Aphrodite 74

Crew..75

Technical Features 76

Famous B-17 Pilots and Crew Members 78

Memphis Belle...85

A page of history..91

Eighth Air Force 93

VIII Bomber Command 97

Combat Box 106

The Bombing of Schweinfurt....................................113

The Aphrodite Project...121

Post-war use..124

Boeing XB-38 Flying Fortress..................................126

Allison V-1710 Engine 128

Boeing YB-40 Flying Fortress..................................131

General characteristics 137

The surviving B-17s..138

Boeing C-108 Flying Fortress 141

B-17 Flying Fortress

"We have the finest bomber in the world."

So published the New York Times on the morning of July 29, 1935, after the Model 299, the progenitor of one of the most famous aircraft of all time, the Boeing B-17 Flying Fortress, had made its maiden flight over Seattle the day before, with Boeing's chief test pilot Leslie R. Tower at the controls.

The Boeing B-17 Flying Fortress was a four-engine aircraft of the heavy bomber class. It was used primarily by the Army Air Forces in strategic bombing campaigns against German industrial, civilian, and military targets.

The 8th Air Force based in England and the 15th Air Force based in Italy joined the RAF Bomber Command in Operation Pointblank, to ensure air superiority over cities, factories, and battlefields in Western Europe. This operation was a preparation for the Normandy landings.

B-17s also participated in operations in the Pacific Theater of World War II, where they conducted raids against Japanese ships and air bases.

The B-17 is considered the first aircraft to be produced in large numbers, and to subsequently evolve into numerous variants.

History

For the competition announced in May 1934 for a multi-engine bomber, Boeing reworked the technique of the civil transport Model 247, taking advantage of the improvements already introduced on the gigantic four-engine bomber Model 294, then under construction with the acronym XBLR-1 (later changed to XB-15) to create a relatively small four-engine but exuberant in engine power and as modern as possible.
The prototype Model 299 (which did not receive the designation XB-17) began flights on July 28, 1935 in Seattle, piloted by Leslie R. Tower, and on August 20 it moved to Wright Field for official tests, covering the 3,400 km of the route in just nine hours, non-stop.
The Model 299 was the progenitor of one of the most famous aircraft of all time, the Boeing B-17 Fortress, known as the Flying Fortress (the adjective Flying was unofficially added by the English, not the Americans). It is natural that in 1935 it should have seemed revolutionary, especially for a war aircraft. But it rather resembled a beautiful civilian aircraft, so much did it please the eye with its tapered shape, shiny duralumin, without protrusions or recesses, the scarlet stripes of the American flag on the very high vertical fin.

Leslie Tower, after landing, had declared:

"Despite its size and weight, the 299 is maneuverable like a fighter. Flying it is a dream, I did not believe that one could, now, build such a fantastic airplane".

The Model 299, immediately designated XB-17 (i.e. experimental bomber B-17) by the Air Corps General Staff, actually offered extraordinary performance in relation to the not very remarkable power of its engines, 4 Pratt & Whitney of just 750 hp each.

With a takeoff weight of about 43,000 pounds (19,500 kg), it could climb to altitudes of up to 8,000 meters, fly non-stop for 5,000 kilometers and easily exceed 400 km/h.

Its bomb load was 4,800 pounds (2,177 kg), more than double that of the Martin B-10, then the Air Corps' standard bomber. Four 12.7 mm machine guns constituted the defensive armament. After further tests in Seattle, the Model 299 finally demonstrated its brilliant qualities three weeks later, on August 20, traveling from west to east for 3,400 kilometers at an average of 375 km/h.

At that same time, the nascent German Luftwaffe was just beginning to outline the twin-engine Heinkel 111 as a bomber plane, born under the false guise of a "fast commercial aircraft"; Japan was also developing modern bombers, also twin-engined, but was still waiting for them; the Soviet Union and France had some real bolts; the British Royal Air Force had in its line the Heyford, biplanes, which pathetically recalled the aircraft of the First World War; Italy was about to face the Ethiopian campaign with the equally antiquated Caproni 133, soon it would have the much more efficient Savoia Marchetti 81, but even with them the Regia Aeronautica could not hope to compete even remotely with the Air Corps' XB-17.

Unfortunately, the Model 299, costing 275,000 dollars, was destroyed in an unfortunate takeoff on October 30, which cost the life of test pilot Leslie Tower.

The crew forgot, in fact, to deactivate a device that blocked the flight surfaces; this device was called "gust lock", and was inserted when the plane was parked on the ground. Because of this oversight, after takeoff the plane began to climb rapidly, stalled and crashed to the ground.

Tower lost his life in the accident and some observers on the ground were injured. The loss of the aircraft was not complete, as parts of the wings were salvaged for use in the later development of machine gun mounting points.

Boeing's hopes of completing the contract were dashed: Chief of Staff Malin Craig cancelled the order for 65 B-17s and ordered 133 Douglas B-18 Bolos.

Despite this incident, the USAAC continued to be impressed with the prototype's performance, and on 17 January 1936 the

Air Corps placed an order for 13 aircraft, taking advantage of a regulatory opportunity.

The aircraft was redesignated YB-17 and later Y1B-17.

The YB-17 featured many improvements over the Model 299, including 930 hp Wright R-1820-39 Cyclone engines.

The new aircraft debuted on December 2 of the same year, and 12 examples were assigned directly to the 2nd Bombardment Group between March 1 and August 5, 1937.

In one of the first missions, three B-17s directed by navigator Lieutenant Curtis LeMay were sent by General Andrews to intercept the Italian ocean liner Rex, which was 980 km from the Atlantic coast, and take photographs. The mission was successful and was widely publicized. The US Navy, however, was not very enthusiastic about the success of the operation, so much so that the 2nd Bomber Group, which had the aircraft in force, was subsequently ordered by the Secretary of War not to exceed 100 miles from the coast.

The thirteenth YB-17 was sent to Ohio, to the Material Division of Wright Field, where it was used only for flight tests.

A fourteenth aircraft (number 37-369), originally built for ground tests of the structure's strength, was upgraded and equipped with turbochargers.

These proved to be problematic and the 1937 test flights were postponed until March of the following year.

The entire United States was crossed from east to west in 12 hours 51 minutes, and from west to east in 10 hours 46 minutes. In February 1938 six 299Bs flew compactly from Miami to Buenos Aires, 8,105 km, in 26 hours 50 minutes, including a stop in Lima.

A B-17, named Honky Tonk Sal, still managed to return from a mission on March 15, 1944, despite massive damage to its tail.

The Air Corps generals had every reason to rejoice: with the B-17 they truly had a strategic weapon without equal. Unfortunately, the traditional rivalry between the Army and the Navy - in the United States the air force was not independent - froze the development of long-range strategic programs for some time. The casus belli broke out the day the Italian ocean liner Rex was peacefully intercepted in the Atlantic, for training, by three Fortresses about 1,200 kilometers from New York.
The admirals of the U.S. Navy protested so vigorously about that "undue interference" in the affairs of the Navy that the Secretary of War expressly ordered the industries to cease production of heavy bombers, allowing the Air Corps to keep only medium and light bombers in line, suitable at most for carrying out tactical actions.

It was madness, with the Second World War now knocking at the door. But the fearful advance of European events changed the shortsighted views of the upper echelons.

In early 1939, Boeing presented the Model 299F (Y1B-17A), which astonished by reaching a maximum speed of 500 kilometers per hour, climbing to 9,200 meters and carrying a load of 5,000 kg at a thousand kilometers at an hourly average of 383 km/h, a world record. By now the days of experiments were over. With all the Xs and Ys removed, the Air Corps Fortresses were now called B-17A and B-17B.

The first aircraft was delivered to the Army on January 31, 1939, and was redesignated B-17A, to indicate the first operational variant. A B-17B flew from Burbank, California, to New York at an average speed of 260 mph.

In November, seven B-17Bs flew from Langley Field to Rio de Janeiro. That was enough to overcome even the snarling envy of the admirals, while Boeing designers insisted on perfecting their prototypes.

On July 21, 1940, as the Battle of Britain was about to begin on this side of the Atlantic without a single four-engine aircraft taking part, the B-17C took to the air for the first time, followed shortly thereafter by the B-17D, which was virtually identical, except for a few variations in the mounting of the six on-board weapons.

These new B-17Cs, soon followed by the 1,200 hp B-17Ds, allowed a top speed of 320 mph, truly formidable, despite their total weight of 49,650 pounds (122,520 kg); the sleek lines of the B-17s made exceptional aerodynamic penetration possible.

From the first Model 299 in 1935 to the last B-17D, a total of 134 aircraft had been built. A pittance, since 12,592 more B-17s were to be built later:

- 512 of the E series.
- 3,400 of the F series.
- 8,680 of the G series.

Before the attack on Pearl Harbor, fewer than 200 B-17s were in service, but production was accelerated, and the B-17 became the first large aircraft to be mass-produced.

The aircraft entered service in every combat zone of World War II, and by the time production ended in May 1945, 12,731 had been built by Boeing, Douglas, and Vega (a subsidiary of Lockheed).

Use

By September 3, 1939, at the outbreak of World War II, the Air Corps had 23 Fortresses.

A year later, the B-17s had their baptism of fire in the skies of Europe, under the British flag. Twenty B-17Cs were handed over by the American government to the RAF Bomber Command in 1941, and the first of them reached Prestwick Air Base from Gander, Newfoundland, on April 14, after a record-breaking flight over the Atlantic lasting 8 hours and 26 minutes.

Bomber Command, headed at the time by Air Marshal Sir Richard Peirse, did not expect much from the Fortresses, which had been created specifically as high-altitude daylight bombers.

British airmen had already experienced the dangers of broadside bombing over Germany, and had long since realized that there was nothing they could do against the Reich's fighters.

It is true that, since night radio navigation instruments were not yet developed, in the darkness even very large surface targets could not be identified, but, at least, fewer people died.

However, in the spring of 1941, only a very few four-engined Stirlings and Halifaxes were available in the Bomber Command Squadrons. It was worth taking advantage of the 20 B-17Cs that had come from America and using them on high-altitude daytime missions: they would have been useful for something, since they had the famous Norden aiming sight on their bows, with which, it was said, it was easy to "stick a bomb into a nine-thousand-meter barrel". Exaggerations, of course, partly because Sir Richard Peirse's crews had been trained to fly and fight on airplanes of a completely different design, partly because the armament of the B-17Cs was insufficient or at least poorly distributed and partly because even with the Norden sight gross errors were made from that prohibitive altitude.

Their first mission took place on July 8, 1941 against the Wilhelmshaven submarine base, the last against the Emden shipyards on September 25.

Kiel, Bremen, Brest, Rotterdam and Oslo were also attacked, always with a failed outcome.

The B-17 piloted by 1st Lt. Lawrence DeLancey who still managed to return to England after a direct hit by anti-aircraft fire that killed two of his crew, during a bombing raid on Cologne, Germany.

At the time, the US Air Corps considered 20,000 feet (6,096 m) to be a high-altitude flight and thus safe from threats from the ground. Consequently, the on-board equipment was designed to operate at the temperatures normally found at that altitude; despite this, the RAF, worried about being intercepted by German fighter aircraft of the time, bombed naval installations from a higher altitude, flying as high as 30,000 feet (9,144 m).

The bombers failed to hit their targets from such a high altitude, also considering the fact that this series of aircraft had as its aiming system not the US Norden aiming system (considered top secret), but an English Sperry system still in development; furthermore, the temperatures at the chosen operating altitude were such as to freeze the mechanisms of the machine guns and this did not cause consequences only because the attacking German fighters failed to perform the correct interception maneuver in the rarefied atmosphere.

On 24 July they attempted to bomb Brest, France, but again they missed their targets completely.

After just 22 missions, and after the RAF had lost eight B-17Cs in combat or in accidents, the survivors of the initial force of 20 B-17Cs were decommissioned by Bomber Command and transferred to the less demanding Coastal Command (which would later purchase 45 B-17Es, 19 B-17Fs and 85 B-17Gs). Four more Fortresses were sent to North Africa and, until March 1942, took part in some night raids against Benghazi and Tobruk. Experience had shown the RAF and the USAAF that the B-17C was not ready for combat and that improved defenses, a larger bomb load, and greater accuracy were needed. These improvements were introduced in subsequent versions. Furthermore, even with these upgrades, only the USAAF wanted to continue using the B-17 as a day bomber. The disastrous experience of the B-17Cs in Europe created consternation and dismay in the United States.

Were these the most beautiful bombers in the world?

What had been lacking in those apparently so perfect machines, capable of climbing much higher than the English four-engined planes and carrying up to 7,400 pounds of bombs (3,356 kg) for 3,000 km?

Apart from the distrust and incompetence of the English in their regard (they overloaded them with explosives, thus significantly reducing speed and maneuverability), they had lacked experience.

The Fortresses had yet to gain experience.

Wonderful from a purely aeronautical point of view, they were much less so from a specifically military point of view.

- The authentic Fortresses would have been those of the E, F and G series, also aesthetically different from the previous ones for their characteristic giant rudder, a little less fast, but armed to the teeth on all sides (13 12.7 mm machine guns), armored here and there, more robust and considerably heavier.

A special B-17E, equipped with 4 Allison engines of 1,425 hp, would have reached 526 km/h, in tests, on May 19, 1943. The series B-17Fs would have proven capable of lifting an internal and external bomb load of 20,800 pounds (9,434 kg). But these tests, in warfare, had an irrelevant meaning.

Boeing B-17 Flying Fortress four-engine bombers in bombing action over Nuremberg.

In reality, the Fortresses of the U.S.A.A.F. (United States Army Air Forces, created as practically independent units on June 20, 1941 from the dissolution of the Air Corps) would always have been content, so as not to compromise their own performance, to carry an offensive load of 2 and a half tons, rarely 3 tons.

With the other four-engine B-24 Liberators, with the twin-engine B-25 Mitchell and B-26 Marauder medium bombers, and with the tactical support of fighter-bombers, they would have rendered an immense service to the Allied cause.

The prototype of the B-17E made its first flight on September 5, 1941. Pearl Harbor was just three months and two days away. That Sunday morning, when the Japanese arrived by surprise, 35 Fortresses were dozing peacefully on the runways and in the hangars of the Hawaiian airports. At least twenty of them were blown to pieces in a few minutes, while by a pure miracle another Squadron of B-17s, coming from California, managed to land under the onslaught of the attack.

Immediately, from the Philippines, the B-17Ds of the 19th Group went into action against Japanese shipping in the Pacific, then the few available Fortresses operated from Mindanao, Java and even Australia.

Attacked and decimated by Japanese Zero fighters, they still managed to hit enemy land and naval targets with very heavy blows, waiting to be replaced by the more modern B-17 Es of the 7th Group, against which even the Zeros would often find themselves in difficulty due to their deadly and concentrated barrage.

On 7 December 1941, a group of twelve B-17s from the 38th (four B-17Cs) and 88th (eight B-17Es) Reconnaissance Squadrons, en route to reinforce units in the Philippines, arrived at Pearl Harbor during the Japanese attack. Co-pilot Leonard "Smitty" Smith Humiston, in B-17C (serial number 40-2049) commanded by Lieutenant Robert H. Richards, thought the gunfire was a U.S. Navy salute to celebrate the arrival of the bombers, but soon realized that a battle was underway.

The Flying Fortress was attacked by Japanese fighter planes, but the crew escaped unharmed, except for one person who suffered abrasions to his hands. The Japanese activities forced the aircraft to abort the landing at Hickam Field and head for Bellows Field, where it overran the runway and was subsequently strafed.

Although initially deemed repairable, bomber 40-2049 received more than 200 machine gun hits and was never restored to flying condition.

Another early Pacific battle took place on December 10, 1941, and saw the first B-17 shot down.

The incident involved aircraft commander Colin Kelly, who is remembered as the first American hero of World War II for sacrificing his life by keeping his burning plane aloft long enough for his crew to abandon the aircraft.

The plane hit the Japanese fast battleship Haruna, and Kelly was awarded the Distinguished Service Cross posthumously. The Japanese ace who shot the B-17, Saburo Sakai, noted that the Fortress was particularly tough.

The 19th Group was covered in glory, earning a Congressional Medal of Honor and seven Distinguished Unit Citations. Most famous among all, for its reckless exploits, the Alexander The Swoose, a Fortress that had as its first pilot Colonel Hank Godman, and equally famous Fortresses Galloping Gus, Typhoon, Madam X, Yankee Doodle Jr., Suzy-Q. Among the American crews, the custom of giving funny and even surrealist names to the aircraft (for example, Swoase is a word that does not exist in the English language, being an improvised cross between Swan and Goose) would never cease.

In the South Asian and Pacific theater, from India to Burma, to the Kuril and Aleutian Islands, the Fortresses often operated at a level of excellence, but did not have the opportunity to fully express their potential because they were unable to bomb what would have been their authentic strategic targets: the industrial objectives of the Japanese metropolitan territory.

They could not reach them from any base, not even by overloading themselves with fuel. Only starting from the second half of 1944, after the entry into service of the brand new B-29s (the Super Fortresses), the Americans were able to hit Tokyo, Osaka, Toyama and the other vital centers of Japan. Up to the atomic mushrooms of Hiroshima and Nagasaki. The weight of the intervention of the B-17s in the Mediterranean theater and continental Europe was infinitely more massive than in the Pacific.

Here too, at first, the tasters were rather timid. Only towards the middle of 1942 was the Eighth Air Army of the USAAF formed in Great Britain, first under the command of General Asa Duncan, then of General Carl Spaatz, then of General Ira Eaker and finally of General Jimmy Doolittle.

And only on August 17th a small formation of 12 B-17s, led by Eaker himself and escorted by 4 Squadrons of British Spitfires, attacked the railway yards of Rouen, while 6 other Fortresses were flying over secondary targets.

Sergeant Kent L. West, tail gunner of one of these aircraft, was the first to succeed in shooting down a German Focke-Wulf 190.

The Air Corps (renamed in 1941 United States Army Air Forces or USAAF) used the B-17 and other bombers to hit targets with the then-secret Norden targeting system, a gyroscopically stabilized electro-mechanical computer. During daylight bombing missions this device was able to determine, based on the bomber's input, the point in space at which the bomb should be released to hit the target.

The bomber essentially took over the flight controls of the aircraft during the attack, maintaining a level attitude until reaching the calculated point. Numerous Groups of the Eighth (the best known: 34th, 91st, 92nd, 94th, 95th, 96th, 97th, 100th, 301st, 303rd, 305th, 306th, 351st, 379th, 381st, 384th, 385th), in the next two and a half years, would have the Fortresses, not counting the Groups equipped with Liberators.

Terrible times were coming for Germany.

Among the protagonists of the huge air battle that was about to unleash on the German landers, after all already tormented at night by the Lancasters and Halifaxes of Bomber Command, there would be famous men, such as the writer Bert Stiles and the film actors James Stewart and Clark Cable.

Eight Congressional Medals of Honor and 31 Distinguished Unit Citations would honor these Groups and these men. Even among the Eighth's Fortresses, many became legendary.

Let's recall some names, since they now belong to aviation history: Yankee Doodle, Big Stuff, Johnny Reb, Baby Doll, Berlin Sleeper, Birmingham Blitzkrieg, Peggy D, Alabama Exterminator, Butcher Schop.

On August 17, 1942, eighteen B-17Es, including Yankee Doodle, piloted by Major Paul Tibbets (the pilot of the Enola Gay who dropped the atomic bomb on Hiroshima a few years later) and Brigadier General Ira Eaker, were escorted by RAF Spitfires in the first raid in Europe against the railroad shunting lines at Rouen-Sotteville, France. The operation was a success, with only minor damage to two planes. But the first major U.S.A.A.F. did not take place until October 9, when a mixed force of 115 B-17s and B-24s, with escorts of over 300 fighters, pounded the Fives-Lille targets.

The English remained skeptical. For eight months they had given up attempts to carry out precision bombing on limited targets - simply because they considered them sterile, indeed, impossible - and had moved on to the so-called "zone bombing" against very large surfaces, cities.

The Americans, on the other hand, still believed in precision raids, and these could only be carried out during the day. But, in order to be able to operate during the day and at reasonable altitudes, that is, between 4,000 and 6,000 meters, despite the formidable armament of the Fortresses and Liberators, fighter protection was needed. And the fighters, because of their limited autonomy, could not accompany the bombers deep over German territory.

Only on January 27, 1943 did the U.S.A.A.F. carry out their first, double raid on the Reich (55 B-17s with 130 tons of bombs on Wilhelmshaven, the B-24s on Emden), but there were still a thousand problems to solve in order to achieve truly significant results to the detriment of the Nazi Moloch.

In the Mediterranean area, the U.S. B-17s began their work of destruction on August 11, 1942, attacking Axis ships in the port of Benghazi. But it was after the landing in Algeria, on November 8, that a terrifying escalation began. On December 4, 20 Liberators visited Naples for the first time. The Fortresses appeared in January 1943 on Palermo, in formations of 24-36 aircraft, then the number of aircraft used in each single raid multiplied.

Cagliari was bombed on March 31 by 99 Fortresses, Naples on April 4 by 91 Fortresses, on May 30 by 130, on July 15 by 154, on July 17 by 97 Fortresses accompanied by another 256 bombers of different types. The cities of Southern and Insular Italy, and later also some cities in the North, were hammered and devastated without respite for months and months. The Americans, it is true, were looking for so-called precision targets, but in reality the bombs fell almost everywhere, like the English ones at night on Milan, Turin and Genoa. It is impossible to even briefly summarize the tragedy. Among the other most destructive raids carried out on Italy mainly by B-17s, the following are worth mentioning:

- on Palermo on May 9
- on Messina on May 25 and June 25
- on Livorno on May 28 and June 26
- on La Spezia on June 5
- on Bologna on July 24 and September 2
- on Foggia on July 22, August 19 and 25, then on September 7
- on Naples on August 4
- on Terni on August 11
- on Pisa on August 31
- on Trento on September 2.

As for Rome, it was hit for the first time on July 19 by 4 Groups of B-17s and 5 Groups of B-24s (a total of 270 four-engined aircraft), and the second time on August 13 by 106 B-17s escorted by 45 P-38 fighters. Even after the armistice of September 8, and until the end of the war, the Fortresses continued to attack Italian territory without interruption, taking advantage of the fact that the Italian skies were much less defended than the German ones.

These Fortresses belonged to the Twelfth Air Army (the Liberators to the Ninth), while in 1944 the Fifteenth was established in Italy and from our bases began to carry out large-scale operations against Germany, in connection with the Eighth stationed in England. Especially in 1943, before the possibilities of penetration of escort fighters extended, Luftwaffe fighters sometimes managed to open real gaps in the B-17 formations.

Terrible was the massacre of October 14, remembered as Black Thursday. That day 291 B-17s took off from various British airfields escorted by 103 P-47s to bomb the ball bearing factories in Schweinfurt. But the P-47s could not accompany the Fortresses to the target and had to leave them alone on the last stretch of the journey, at the mercy of the Messerschmitt 109s and Focke-Wulf 190s.

The German fighters gathered in their hundreds in the Frankfurt area, then launched an attack using a system already adopted on some occasions over Sicily: they launched 30-millimeter rockets from a great distance to disjoin the formations, then threw themselves on the isolated aircraft, attacking them head-on, to avoid the simultaneous barrage.

Although attacked from all sides, the Americans still reached Schweinfurt and 228 B-17s dropped 358 tons of explosive bombs and 80 tons of incendiary bombs. But, out of 291 aircraft that took off, 60 were destroyed and another 138 suffered such serious damage that they were immediately cancelled by the Eighth Air Force.

The blood toll paid by the crews was enormous if one considers that each B-17 carried 10 men and that, apart from the sixty that were shot down, many aircraft returned with dead on board. The situation gradually improved as the escort fighters' autonomy increased.

In August 1943, P-47 Thunderbolts equipped with supplementary tanks, starting from English bases, could reach at most just beyond the Bremen-Hanover-Kassel-Frankfurt line, but already in November the P-38 Lightning were capable of penetrating beyond Stuttgart-Nuremberg-Leipzig and as far as Berlin, while by early 1944 the P-51 Mustangs controlled all of German territory.

Only then was Germany lost, despite the considerable strength of its ground and air defense.

With the cities scourged one by one by Bomber Command at night, with the most vital objectives devastated by the Eighth and Fifteenth U.S.A.A.F. by day, the Third Reich was inevitably heading for collapse.

By October 1943, the Fortresses' bombers were already able to place about 25% of their bombs within a radius of 300 meters of the target and almost 50% within a radius of 600 meters. Later, they achieved even better results. The skies of Germany were blacked out for more than a year, literally, by fleets of 500-800 and even 1,000 or more American bombers.

- Berlin was hit for the first time by B-17s - about thirty - on March 4, 1944, but just two days later, 627 of these "beautiful" but now frightening aircraft swarmed over its streets and squares, over 22 meters long, with a wingspan of 31 meters and 64, with a total weight that often exceeded 27 tons.

- The two heaviest American assaults on Berlin were on February 3, 1945, when 937 B-17s dropped 2,054 tons of bombs, and on February 26, when 1,112 B-17s and B-24s dropped another 2,618 tons.

By now the lines of communication, oil refineries, aircraft factories, chemical plants, shipyards, missile bases, hydrogenation plants and all other primary targets had virtually ceased to exist in Germany, buried under mountains of high explosives. In the European theater the B-17s dropped a total of 580,875 tons of bombs, compared with 410,488 tons for the Liberators and 420,520 tons for all other types of U.S.A.A.F. aircraft; only the Lancasters of Bomber Command, with their 618,378 tons, exceeded the Fortresses in the amount of explosives dropped. After examining the wreckage of B-17s and B-24s, Luftwaffe officers discovered that it took at least 20 rounds from a .79-inch (20.1 mm) cannon to shoot down a B-17 bomber from behind.

Most skilled pilots hit enemy aircraft with only 2 percent of their shells, so to hit a bomber with 20 shots, a pilot would have to fire about a thousand rounds. Early versions of the Focke-Wulf 190, one of Germany's best interceptors, were equipped with two 20 mm MG FF machine guns, each with only 500 rounds.

Later versions used the MG 151 cannon, which had a longer range but was still effective at no more than 400 meters, while the shells fired from the B-17 turrets were lethal at up to 1,000 meters. For this reason, German aircraft were at a disadvantage with the tactic of approaching from behind.

The Germans found that there was a greater advantage in attacking head-on, both because fewer defensive guns were deployed and because the bomber could be shot down with only four or five hits. To improve the offensive deficiencies of the FW 190, the number of guns was increased from two to four, and the amount of ammunition carried was also increased. In 1944, a further upgrade was made to the 1.2-inch (30.5 mm) MK 108 gun, which could down a B-17 with just a few hits.

The Luftwaffe was among the operators of the B-17; initially a single aircraft forced into a belly landing in December 1942 was repaired and handed over to I/KG.200, a special unit dedicated to clandestine operations. In the following months, two more aircraft were captured and restored to flying condition; the aircraft was redesignated with the cover name Dornier Do 200. The aircraft were used to airdrop agents behind the lines for the remainder of the war on various fronts, from Ireland to Algeria and the Middle East. Only one of the German Flying Fortresses survived and was recaptured at Altenburg after the armistice.

A so-called "Cheyenne" tail turret, named after the factory where it was first installed starting with the B-17G variants.

The American government refused to sell B-17s to the Soviet Union.
Despite this, at least 73 Flying Fortresses (Boeing model 299-0) were used by the Soviet Air Force.
These were mostly aircraft that had been forced to land after the famous "shuttle" bombings on the Third Reich or damaged during a Luftwaffe attack on Poltava airfield.
Twenty-three B-17s were restored to flying condition by Russian technicians but never saw combat. They were concentrated in the 45th BAD / 890th BAP which in 1946 was assigned to the Kazan aircraft factory to support the production of the Tupolev Tu-4, a copy of the Boeing B-29.

Operation Pointblank

The two different strategies of the British and American commands were organized at the Casablanca Conference in January 1943, where Operation Pointblank was planned, to weaken the Wehrmacht and establish air superiority in preparation for the ground offensive.
Operation Pointblank began with attacks on targets in Western Europe. General Eaker and the Eighth Air Force set as priority targets the German aircraft industries, especially the fighter aircraft assembly plants, the engine factories and the ball bearing manufacturers.
On 17 April 1943, an attack on the Focke-Wulk factory in Bremen, carried out by 115 B-17s, had little success: sixteen Flying Fortresses were shot down and 48 others were damaged. Nevertheless, the attack succeeded in distracting half of the Luftwaffe forces in anti-bomb operations.
Since the bombing of air bases was not appreciably reducing Germany's air power, additional B-17 groups were formed and Eaker ordered missions deeper into enemy territory against important industrial targets.
The Eighth Air Force targeted ball bearing factories in Schweinfurt, hoping to damage war production. The first raid on 17 August 1943 did not cause critical damage to the factories and the 230 B-17 bombers were intercepted by approximately 300 Luftwaffe fighters.
As a result, 36 bombers were shot down with the loss of 200 crewmen and together with the losses from the raids on Regensburg, a total of 60 B-17s were lost that day.
A second attempt on 14 October 1943 would later be known as "Black Thursday".
Of the 291 bombers, 59 were shot down over Germany, one crashed in the English Channel, five crashed in England, and 12 were damaged or crashed, for a total loss of 77 aircraft. Another 122 were damaged and required repairs before they could return to the air.

Of the 2,900 airmen who had been part of the crews, 650 did not return, although some survived as prisoners of war. Of the damaged aircraft that did return, there were 5 killed and 43 wounded crew members.

Only 33 aircraft landed safely. All of these losses were caused by concentrated attacks by over 300 German fighter aircraft. These losses were unsustainable, and the USAAF, recognizing the vulnerability of unescorted heavy bombers, suspended daylight bombing raids over German territory until escort aircraft could be developed to protect the B-17s on their way from England to Germany and back. The Eighth Air Force lost 176 aircraft in October 1943, and on 11 January 1944, it suffered heavy losses on missions to Oschersleben, Halberstadt, and Braunschweig. Doolittle called off the mission that day due to bad weather, but the lead units had already entered enemy airspace and continued the mission.

Most of the escort aircraft turned back or missed the rendezvous, resulting in 60 B-17s being destroyed.

The third raid on Schweinfurt on 24 February 1944 was remembered as the "Big Week". Using P-51 Mustangs and P-47 Thunderbolts (with drop tanks to increase range), the B-17s were adequately protected from the enemy, and only 11 of 231 bombers were shot down. Escort aircraft reduced losses to less than 7 percent, and only 247 B-17s were lost in 3,500 flights. By September 1944, 27 of the 40 groups that made up the Eighth Air Force and six of the 21 groups in the Fifteenth Air Force were operating B-17s.

Losses from antiaircraft guns continued to be high throughout 1944, but by 27 April 1945 (two days after the last heavy bombing mission in Europe), losses had fallen so low that replacement aircraft were no longer needed, and the number of bombers in each group was reduced. The coordinated bombing offensive was effectively over.

Norden targeting system

The Norden was a gyroscopically stabilized electro-mechanical computer used on bombers by the United States Army Air Forces during World War II and later by the United States Air Force in the Vietnam and Korean wars to locate the exact point at which to drop bombs.

- The mechanism of operation of this device was kept a secret by the United States throughout World War II.

However, Herman Lang, a German spy who worked in the factory where the Norden was produced, managed to deliver some blueprints of the machine to the Abwehr in 1938.

As a result, starting in 1942, the German company Carl Zeiss began to deliver similar devices to the Luftwaffe, called Lotfernrohr 7.

- The Norden was designed for use on United States Navy aircraft by Dutch engineer Carl Norden, who had studied in Switzerland, and then moved to the United States in 1904. The Norden was usually mounted on the nose of the aircraft, so as to lock onto the target during the approach to it.

Once the target was locked, the mechanism inside the Norden ensured that it remained continuously centered on the same point as the aircraft approached, taking into account the altitude and speed of the aircraft, so as to signal the exact moment to release the bombs.

- One of the major problems that all air forces faced during World War II was the difficulty of hitting a moving ship with bombers.

In an attempt to solve this problem, most belligerent states invested heavily in dive bombing and torpedo bombers, but these aircraft generally had a rather limited range and could only be used if carried on aircraft carriers. Instead, the US military focused on the Norden mounted on Boeing B-17 Flying Fortress bombers, which were believed to have sufficient accuracy and could guarantee a much greater range, taking off from land-based air bases.

- Using the Norden, these bombers could, theoretically, drop their bombs in a circle about 30 meters in diameter from an altitude of 7,000 meters, a height sufficient to keep the bombers away from the danger of carrier-based anti-aircraft guns.

In reality, the Norden failed to achieve anywhere near the accuracy its creators had hoped for.
The Royal Air Force (RAF) was the first to use B-17s in warfare and achieved poor results, so much so that the bombers were converted to other functions. The United States Army Air Forces (USAAF) operations in the Pacific to hit Japanese ships also generally ended in failure. In fact, although numerous sinkings were reported, the only known successful operation occurred during the Japanese invasion of the Philippines, when a minesweeper was sunk and two Japanese transport ships were damaged.
However, this operation was an exception to the rule, given the repeated failures during the Battle of the Coral Sea and the Battle of Midway.
Eventually, the USAAF also replaced the B-17s with other bombers.
Dense clouds were a constant over Europe and led to a worsening of the Norden's accuracy, which was already having serious difficulties operating in clear skies.

- It was demonstrated that in Europe, under perfect atmospheric conditions, only 50% of the bombs dropped exploded within 400 meters of the target selected with the Norden; furthermore, American pilots calculated that approximately 90% of the bombs dropped failed to hit the target.

Since the mechanism behind the Norden was considered a top secret, the pilots of bombers equipped with this instrument were required, during their training, to swear an oath to defend the machine with their lives, if necessary.

If the pilot had to make an emergency landing in enemy territory, he had to shoot the most important parts of the machine, in order to render it unusable. To ensure that no machine could fall into enemy hands intact, the pilots were equipped with thermite-based ammunition, capable of turning the Norden into a useless pile of metal.

The Norden targeting system.

As the war progressed, the secret of the Norden was gradually declassified, until 1944, when a schematic of the machine's operation was published. During a trip to Germany in 1938, the German spy Herman Lang conferred with the German military authorities and together with them reconstructed the plans for the Norden, which he had carefully memorized. In 1942 he was arrested by the FBI along with 32 other German agents: he was sentenced to 18 years in prison on charges of espionage.

The Sperry Spherical Turret

The B-17's spherical turret was a small, one-man cockpit equipped with a pair of .50-caliber Browning machine guns and mounted with a mechanical altazimuth movement system very similar to that of telescopes.

- The spherical turret could rotate 360 degrees in the horizontal plane of the plane (azimuth) and 90 degrees in the perpendicular plane; in short, it covered virtually every angle from the belly down.

The turret was very small and light to limit the already very heavy load that weighed on the bomber.

It was usually operated by the smallest member of the crew, who found himself with the unenviable task of standing for hours in the suffocating and tiny spherical cabin while German fighters whistled around him.

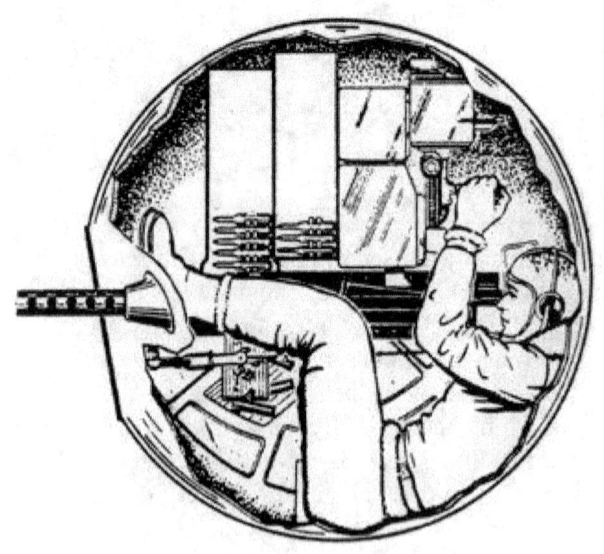

To get inside the turret, you had to crouch down and assume a fetal position. Once inside, there was no room to move, much less room to put a parachute inside. If the turret came loose for any reason, the gunner would fly down with it.

• There was no room for ammunition in the turret either.

The Browning machine guns were loaded from the belly of the plane, above. Operating a pair of MGs simultaneously was not an opportunity that came along every day. The operator of the Sperry spherical turret had two directional controls, one in each hand, with integrated fire controls.
In short, the classic joystick with which the gunner could rotate the turret and shoot.

Technique

The Boeing B-17 was a four-engine, low-wing cantilever aircraft of all-metal construction, with cruciform empennage of considerable surface area and a fully retractable tricycle rear landing gear. The wing was on symmetrical biconvex profiles. Its structure was based on two longerons with tubular light alloy soles, connected by a lattice of riveted diagonals, as well as on a dense camber, also in lattice. The covering was in avional sheets, stiffened by an internal planking in corrugated sheet metal. The two half-wings were directly connected, by means of high-strength steel attachments, to the sides of the fuselage, whose maximum diameter was approximately double the thickness that the wing presented at the root, and each of them was divided into three distinct elements:
- The internal trunk, with the two engine nacelles and the landing gear leg.
- The external section, on which the canvas aileron extended, with maximum angles of $\pm\,12°$.
- The terminal connection.

The wing was equipped with large constant chord split flaps, which at the maximum angle of 45° reduced the stall speed by about fifteen kilometers per hour. The wing structure was remarkably light, weighing about 20 kg per square meter, and was also extremely robust, being able to absorb even significant damage without giving way.

The fuselage, with a circular section, was made up of a complex of nine elements:
- The bow.
- The nose.
- The section housing the cockpit.
- The central section incorporating the bomb bay.
- The center-rear section.
- The rear conical section, the one to which the empennage was attached.
- The terminal cone, with the tail gunner's position.

- The element that covered the cockpit.
- And connected it to the back of the fuselage.

The fuselage structure was based on a dense series of Z-section diaphragms, on three robust double-T extruded longerons (two dorsal and one ventral), and on numerous L-shaped stiffening stringers.

The horizontal empennage, with a trapezoidal plan, and the vertical one, with the characteristic fin, had a completely metal structure on the fixed surfaces, and covered in canvas for the mobile ones.

The rudder and the two semi-balancers, similarly to the left aileron, were equipped with corrector flaps, while the leading edge of the fixed surfaces and that of the external half-wings and the wing sections between the internal and external engine nacelles were equipped with sheaths for pneumatic de-icing.

The front legs of the landing gear, equipped with oleopneumatic shock absorbers and wheels of 1.424 meters in diameter, with covers on sixteen layers, retracted electrically into the internal driving nacelles, with rotation towards the front, without however hiding completely. The tail wheel, placed in a rather advanced position, retracted into the belly of the fuselage, rotating towards the rear.

- The engines of the B-17G were the Wright «Cyclone» R-1820 nine-cylinder star engines, with reduction gear, Bendix injection carburetor and General-Electric B 22 exhaust gas turbochargers, equipped with Minneapolis-Honeywell electronic control systems, installed in the belly of the driving nacelles, and which received the air for the engine supply and for the inter-refrigeration groups from the intakes arranged in the wing leading edge.

The engines were installed in aerodynamically well-profiled nacelles, attached to steel tube engine mounts, and were isolated from the aircraft by sheet steel firewalls. They drove three-bladed Hamilton Standard constant-speed propellers of 3.53 metres in diameter, with feathering capability and liquid runway de-icing.

- An important development was the use of turbochargers on the engines of the new bombers, in order to evaluate the possibility of flying at higher altitudes, with a lower risk of interception.

Considerable problems had to be solved in the arrangement and layout of the compressors and other auxiliary equipment before being able to proceed with flight tests.

The positioning of the turbochargers above the engine cowling caused a high level of turbulence, generating among other things considerable vibrations and, after a series of negative tests, Boeing, at its own expense, placed them under the fairings, a position then adopted up to the latest production models.

- The turbochargers allowed the ceiling to be raised by 3,000 meters and the speed by over 60 km/h.

The fuel system was always, on all B-17s, perhaps the least satisfactory part, proving to be quite vulnerable to enemy attacks. It consisted of, in addition to the various pipes, pumps, valves, filters and control organs, twenty-four wing tanks (two arranged between the sides of the fuselage and the internal engine nacelles, four between the engine nacelles, and eighteen externally to these), all of the self-sealing type, to which could be added the supplementary tanks installed in the bomb bay for long-distance flights, which brought the total capacity of the system from 10,533 to 13,627 litres.

The lubricant, for a total of 560 litres, was contained in four self-sealing tanks, installed in the engine nacelles behind the firewall.

- The electrical system was particularly well-finished, and most of the on-board utilities were connected to it, including the actuators for the flaps, the bomb bay doors, and those for lowering and retracting the landing gear.

The wheel brakes and the flaps for regulating engine cooling were instead controlled by the hydraulic system.

Considerable attention had been paid to the problem of ensuring easy and safe use of the aircraft even over long distances and at maximum altitudes, and the B-17 (model G) had, in fact, an autopilot, four separate networks for inhaling gaseous oxygen and a heating system powered by a glycol heat exchanger, installed in the left internal engine nacelle.

The radio equipment for communications and navigation was also highly developed, and the aircraft was also equipped with an intercom system for the crew.

- The defensive armament of the B-17G was certainly among the most effective and best studied of all those installed on the bombers of the Second World War, and was based on 13 12.7 mm machine guns, two placed in each of the tail, dorsal, ventral and front turrets, under the transparent nose.

To these eight weapons were added the two lateral ones, for the defense of the sides of the fuselage, the dorsal one (often absent) placed in the radio operator's compartment, and the two installed in the sides of the nose.

The bomb load, except in short-range missions, was on the other hand rather limited, usually not exceeding 2,500 kg, even if (rather rarely) the application of bomb racks under the wing root allowed the offensive load to be brought to 9,454 kg, in short-range missions.

The Norden gyroscopic aiming sight, installed in the transparent nose, allowed good shooting precision, even if the use of the Boeing bomber in numerous formations (whose components dropped simultaneously on the target) and from high altitudes constantly went to the detriment of the aiming precision.

- Finally, the aircraft was equipped with abundant armor for the protection of the crew.

The bombers could not maneuver effectively to evade enemy fighter attacks, and during the final approach to the target, aiming and releasing the bombs (bombing run) they had to fly straight and level, leaving them exposed to direct attack.

A US Army Air Force survey conducted in 1943 showed that over half of the bombers shot down by the Germans had left the protection of the main formation.

- To mitigate the problem, the United States developed better bombing formation techniques, which evolved into staggered battle groups where all the B-17s could safely cover each other with machine guns.

In this way, a bomber formation became a dangerous target to engage. The bomber battle formation was, however, very rigid and vulnerable to German anti-aircraft weapons.

In addition, Luftwaffe fighter pilots, known as "Jagdflieger", developed the counter-tactic of making rapid fire passes, avoiding engaging individual bombers.

- As a result, the B-17 loss rate rose to 25% in the first missions (60 of 291 B-17s were lost in combat in the second raid on Schweinfurt).

Only with the advent of long-range escort aircraft (especially the North American P-51 Mustang), which countered the action of Luftwaffe interceptors, between February and June 1944, did B-17 missions assume strategic significance.

- From the beginning of the air campaign, B-17s stood out for their ability to take damage during combat and to succeed in reaching the target and returning the crew to base.
- Wally Hoffman, a B-17 pilot in the Eighth Air Force, said, "The airplane can be cut and torn almost to pieces by enemy fire and will bring the crew home."

Marin Caidin reported an incident in which a B-17 collided in mid-air with a Focke-Wulf Fw 190, lost an engine, and suffered damage to both starboard horizontal stabilizers and the vertical stabilizer, in addition to falling out of formation.

Some observers reported that the aircraft was badly damaged and nearly lost its tail, but it managed to stay aloft and return its crew to base.

- Its ability to take hits made up for its inferior range and payload to the B-24 Liberator or the British Avro Lancaster.

Reports abounded of B-17s returning to base with their tails destroyed, or with only one engine functioning, or with large portions of their wings damaged by flak.

- Its ruggedness, combined with the large numbers of aircraft in service with the Eighth Air Force and the fame of the Memphis Belle, made the B-17 a significant aircraft in World War II.

The design underwent eight major modifications during its production, culminating in the B-17G model.

The latter differed from its predecessor by the addition of a turret with two .50-inch (12.7 mm) Browning M2 machine guns under the aircraft's nose. These additional weapons eliminated the main defensive weakness, which was frontal attacks. An important role in the mass bombing missions was played by some aircraft equipped with electronic fire control equipment. These aircraft, the so-called pathfinders, detected the position of the target on the ground even in case of cloud cover and directed the rest of the raid by marking the area with smoke signals, since the American raids were carried out during the day, while the British were at night.

The instruments were progressively refined; the first was Gee, a short-range navigation instrument; then came Oboe, which used signals emitted by ground stations in British territory, so that their intersection and the angle of emission gave the position of the target, like the German X-Gerät.

Oboe was used for the first time in December 1941.

The Oboe system used two ground transmitting stations, positioned in British territory in two separate and distant sites.

- One had the task of providing indications on the route and any corrections, the other reported that the point previously established for the release of the bombs on the target had been reached.

The signals were received by a specially equipped de Havilland Mosquito, which acted as a target indicator.

Once the position of the target was determined, it was retransmitted to the bombers.

The two transmitting stations were codenamed Mouse and Cat. Initially Mouse was positioned in Cromer and Cat in Dover. Both constantly followed the path of a Mosquito equipped with a transponder.

- The transponder retransmitted the received signals and the time difference between transmission and reception, calculated in England, gave the distance from each of the two stations.

Each of the Oboe stations used the distance information to define a circle of known radius. The intersection of the two circles was the position of the aircraft. The Mosquito flew along the circle controlled by the Cat station and, if it deviated from the course, the pilot received instructions to return to the optimal path.

Ventral turret.

When the intersection with the circle calculated by the Mouse was reached, the aircraft would drop its bombs or markers to mark the position, visible to other bombers.

Then came H2S, a ground-scanning radar placed in a sort of tub under the nose, and its successor H2X, in a hemispherical radome placed under the fuselage, behind the wing in place of the ventral turret.

H2S was used for the first time during a raid on Emden on 27 September 1943, when the first part of the formation guided by pathfinders and the second, guided by the smoke released by these, succeeded in hitting the city, while the third part, which had bombed by sight in a break in the clouds, put the bombs miles off target.

- Another device was Carpet, an emitter of radar jamming of English creation, which was airborne and was very effective in jamming the anti-aircraft guidance radars.

At the end of the war, a number of USAAF B-17Gs were converted to the search and rescue role as the B-17H, after being fitted with a maritime search radar in a radome under the nose and an inflatable rescue boat in the bomb bay. The U.S. Navy also used it, but for the AEW role, after having fitted it with an APS-20 radar and redesignated it PB-1W.

- According to aviators of the time, the least coveted position was that of the ventral gunner or the upper gunner.

The upper surface of the B-17 was subjected to constant strafing by Luftwaffe fighters, this was often the most effective technique, attacking from above or below gave a larger surface to hit, or the wings, which contained the fuel, a series of well-placed hits to the wings, and the B-17s turned into fireballs in the sky. The lower part was also subject to fighter incursions or even worse to enemy anti-aircraft fire; the ventral turret often jammed or became inexorably damaged and it was no longer possible to recover the operator, also because in the event of a landing with a damaged landing gear (60% of cases found) due to the hits suffered, he would have been crushed. The mechanism that retracted it onto the belly of the fuselage was often unreliable due to a drop in hydraulic pressure.

Wright R-1820 Engine

The Wright R-1820 Cyclone 9 was one of the most widely used radial engines produced in the United States in the period from 1930 to 1950.

The Cyclone was born as a development of an earlier radial engine produced by Wright. In 1919, the Wright Aeronautical Corporation was founded, an American company that dealt with the production of Hispano-Suiza aeronautical engines built under license. The first independent project was the Wright R-1, an engine that was very successful and that laid the foundation for the creation of a unit that met the specifications of the request of the U.S. Navy for a new air-cooled radial engine.

This led to the design in 1924 of the Wright P-2, predecessor of the Cyclone, never brought into production due to the resignation of the design engineer Frederick Rentschler, who together with his staff preferred to accept the proposals of the competitor Pratt & Whitney.

However, in 1927 Wright Aeronautical began production of the R-1820, which was so successful that it was mounted on several aircraft during the 1930s.

In 1929 the company merged with Curtiss to form Curtiss-Wright. After this merger, a more powerful version of this engine began to be developed that could reach a power of 1,000 hp (746 kW).

- From this project came the R-1820, whose production began in 1935 and which would become one of the most used engines in the 1930s and in World War II.

The R-1820 was also built under license by Lycoming Engines, Pratt & Whitney Canada and also, during World War II, by Studebaker.

The Soviet Union also purchased the rights to produce it under license, designating it the M-25, and established a design bureau, OKB 19, headed by engineer Arkady Dmitrievič Švecov to further develop that project.

The R-1820 powered many well-known aircraft, including Douglas' early airliners (from the prototype DC-1, DC-2, the first civilian versions of the famous DC-3, up to the limited production of the DC-5), probably the best-known US bomber, the Boeing B-17 Flying Fortress, the Douglas SBD Dauntless dive bomber, early versions of the Soviet Polikarpov I-16 fighter (with the aforementioned M-25), and the Piasecki H-21 helicopter.

The R-1820 also had an interesting, if limited, use in powering tanks. The G-200 version was a gasoline-powered version of the 9-cylinder radial engine that developed 900 hp (660 kW) at 2,300 rpm installed on the M6 tank. Caterpillar Inc. converted the Wright RD-1820 to diesel operation, designating it the D-200, which developed 450 hp (300 kW) at 2,000 rpm; this powered the M4A6 Sherman tank.

Characteristics

- Engine type: 9-cylinder radial aircraft engine, aluminum alloy crankcase consisting of two main blocks connected by bolts, steel cylinders with forged pistons and light alloy (bolted) heads, pusher crank mechanism with main connecting rod and secondary connecting rods with an H-section; crankshaft made of two forged parts of nickel-chromium steel with two main bearings for cylindrical roller bearings.
- Cooling: air.
- Fuel system: petrol, with a double-barrel Stromberg injection carburetor upstream of the compressor and equipped with an automatic fuel-air mixture regulator.
- Distribution: 2 overhead valves per cylinder controlled by rods and rockers, the exhaust valves are cooled internally with sodium salts.
- Compressor: mechanically controlled centrifugal, driven by the crankshaft, single-stage and two speeds, with a compression ratio of 7.21:1 at low speed and 10.14:1 at high speed.
- Ignition system: two spark plugs per cylinder powered by two independent distributor magnets.
- Lubrication system: forced, with a delivery gear pump and a recovery pump from the crankcase.
- Propeller reduction ratio: 0.666 via planetary reduction gear with spur gears
- Length: 1,201 mm (47.2 in)
- Diameter: 1,400 mm (55.1 in)
- Displacement: 29.88 L (1,823 in^3). The R-1820 designation identifies the model based on its displacement in cubic inches, approximately 1,820 in^3.
- Bore: 155.6 mm (6.1 in)
- Stroke: 174 mm (6.9 in)
- Compression ratio - 6.8:1
- Empty weight: 605 kg (1,300 lb)

- Power: 1,300 hp (970 kW) at 1,220 m (3,900 ft) at 2,600 rpm. 1,000 hp (745 kW) at 5,330 m (17,500 ft) at 2,600 rpm.
- Power-to-weight ratio: 1.60 kW/kg
- Fuel: 90 octane gasoline
- Lubrication: dry sump with a pressure pump and a recycling pump.

A special version was the R-1820-97 equipped with a turbocharger in addition to the centrifugal compressor for a power of 1,200 hp (895 Kw).

Versions

The B-17 underwent several modifications at each stage of development and during production. Of the 13 YB-17s ordered for testing, 12 were used to develop heavy bombing techniques, while the thirteenth was used for flight testing. This led to the development of turbochargers, which were later used in aircraft. A fourteenth aircraft, the Y1B-17A, was originally designed only for ground testing, but was upgraded with turbochargers. Once upgraded, it was designated the B-17A, and in April 1938, it was the first aircraft to enter service with the designation B-17.
As the production line developed, Boeing engineers continued to develop the basic design.
To increase performance at low speeds, the B-17B was developed, which included a larger rudder and flaps. The B-17C featured modified teardrop-shaped windows, which were flat to eliminate the turbulence created by the earlier blister turrets.
The B-17E version had a 10-foot (3 m) longer fuselage, a larger vertical fin and rudder.
A tail gun emplacement was also added, and the nose was modified. The engines were upgraded to more powerful versions several times, and the gunners' emplacements were similarly modified on several occasions to improve their effectiveness.
By the time the final B-17G appeared, the number of machine guns had been increased from seven to thirteen, and the emplacement designs were completed.
The B-17G was the final version of the B-17, incorporating all of the changes made to the previous model, the B-17F.
8,680 were built, the last on 9 April 1945. Many B-17Gs were converted for other missions, such as cargo transport, engine testing, and reconnaissance. Some B-17Gs, redesignated SB-17Gs, were converted for search and rescue duties, later redesignated B-17Hs.
The XB-38 and YB-40 prototypes were developed from the B-17s.

The XB-38 was used to test the Allison V-1710 liquid-cooled engines. The YB-40 was a heavily armed version of the standard bomber used before the development of the P-51 Mustang, a long-range fighter aircraft. Additional armament included a twin dorsal turret occupying the radio bay, a twin nose turret, and two machine guns in the side emplacements instead of the single gun of the standard version.

The armament thus reached a total of 14 machine guns. The ammunition load was over 11,000 rounds and all the war equipment made this variant about 4,500 kg heavier than a fully loaded B-17F model. In fact, the YB-17 had difficulty keeping up with the standard bombers without a load so, with the advent of the P-51 Mustang, the project was abandoned in July 1943.

Model 299

The Model 299, immediately designated XB-17 (i.e. B-17 experimental bomber) by the Air Corps General Staff, actually offered extraordinary performance in relation to the not very remarkable power of its engines, 4 Pratt & Whitney of just 750 hp each.

The prototype was in fact powered by four Pratt & Whitney Hornet S1E-G nine-cylinder, air-cooled, supercharged radial engines, with a displacement of 1,690.537 cubic inches (27.703 liters) and a compression ratio of 6.5:1.

- The S1E-G was rated at 750 horsepower (560 kW) at 2,250 rpm and 875 horsepower at 2,300 rpm for takeoff, using 87 octane gasoline.

In flight tests, the Model 299 had a cruising speed of 204 miles per hour (328 kilometers per hour) and a maximum speed of 236 miles per hour (380 kilometers per hour) at 10,000 feet (3,048 meters).

Its ceiling was 24,620 feet (7,504.20 meters).

Its maximum range was 3,101 miles (4,991 kilometers).

- Its bomb load was 4,000 pounds, eight 500-pound bombs (eight 500-pound bombs for a total of 4,000 pounds), double that of the Martin B-10, then the Air Corps' standard bomber, with a range of 2,040 miles (3,283 kilometers).

The prototype had a defensive armament of five half-inch (12.7 mm) Browning M2 air-cooled machine guns:

- One in the nose turret.
- One dorsal.
- One ventral.
- One on each side of the fuselage.

After further tests in Seattle, the Model 299 finally demonstrated its brilliant qualities three weeks later, on August 20, by traveling from west to east for 3,400 km at an average speed of 375 km/h.

At that same time, the nascent German Luftwaffe was just beginning to outline the twin-engine Heinkel 111 as a bomber aircraft, born under the false guise of a "fast commercial aircraft"; Japan was also building modern bombers, also twin-engined, but was still waiting for them; the Soviet Union and France possessed some real bolts; the British Royal Air Force had in its line the Heyford, biplanes, which pathetically recalled the aircraft of the First World War; Italy was about to face the Ethiopian campaign with the equally antiquated Caproni 133, and would soon have the much more efficient Savoia Marchetti 81, but even with them the Regia Aeronautica could not hope to even remotely compete with the XB-17 of the Air Corps.

The 299 model (X13372) began with a sleek looking shark fin tail and gun bubbles on the fuselage. It was not until the E model that the tail was enlarged with a huge dorsal fin, creating the classic B-17 look commonly recognized today..

Unfortunately, the $275,000 Model 299 was destroyed in a botched takeoff on October 30, 1935, which cost the life of chief test pilot Leslie Ralph Tower; the cause was quickly identified, attributable to a maneuvering error by the crew and not to a defect in the aircraft.

Despite this, in fact, on January 17, 1936 the Air Corps ordered 13 more prototypes from Boeing, equipped with more powerful 930 hp Wright-Cyclone engines.

Front turret fitted on the Model 299 prototype.

Called model 299B or Y1B-17, it debuted on December 2 of the same year, 13 examples built, of which 12 examples were assigned directly to the 2nd Bombardment Group between March 1 and August 5, 1937.

The crews of Colonel Robert Olds, an old wolf of the air, commander of the Langley Field base, were enthusiastic about having been chosen to test those aircraft that, among themselves, they had already christened Fortresses, not imagining, however, what meaning this name would have, a few years later, for the populations of the countries controlled by the Axis Powers.

Boeing Y1B-17 Flying Fortress 36-149.

The 2nd Group soon gained legendary fame, flying over 2,800,000 km in 9,293 hours on the 299Bs, by day and by night, often in prohibitive weather conditions - the aircraft boasted cutting-edge instrumentation - in all climates, without a single major mechanical accident. Records were also set.

The entire territory of the United States was crossed from east to west in 12 hours and 51 minutes, and from west to east in 10 hours and 46 minutes.

In February 1938, six 299Bs flew compactly from Miami to Buenos Aires - 8,105 km - in 26 hours and 50 minutes, including a stop in Lima. The Air Corps generals had every reason to rejoice: with the B-17 they truly had a strategic weapon without equal.

The engines were changed from the original Pratt & Whitney Hornet radials to Wright FR-1830-39s.

It had a crew of 6.

Technical Features

- Length: 20.82 m (68 ft 4 in).
- Wingspan: 31.63 m (103 ft 9⅜ in).
- Overall height: 5.59 m (18 ft 4 in).
- Empty weight: 11,097 kg (24,465 lb).
- Gross weight: 15,821 kg (34,880 lb).
- Maximum takeoff weight: 19,323 kg (42,600 lb).
- Engines: Four Wright Aeronautical Division Cyclone G59 (R-1820-51) nine-cylinder radial engines of 1,823.129 cubic inches (29.876 L) air-cooled and supercharged with a compression ratio of 6.45:1.
- Power: The R-1820-51 had a normal power rating of 800 hp (800 kW) at 2,100 rpm at sea level and 1,000 hp (1,000 kW) at 2,200 rpm for takeoff, burning 100-octane gasoline.
- Propellers: The engines drove three-bladed Hamilton Standard constant-speed propellers via a gear ratio reduction of 0.6875:1.
- Maximum speed: 412 km/h (256 mph) at 4,267 m (14,000 ft).
- Cruising speed: 412 km/h (217 mph).
- Service ceiling: 9,327 m (30,600 ft).
- Range: 5,343 km (3,320 mi).

- Armament: Five air-cooled .30 caliber Browning machine guns and 8,000 lb (3,629 kg) of bombs.

A long carburetor intake on top of the engine nacelles visually distinguished the YB1-17 from the later YB1-17A.

Y1B-17A

In early 1939, Boeing introduced the Model 299F (Y1B-17A), which astonished by achieving:
- A maximum speed of 501 km/h (311 mph)
- Climbing to 9,200 meters (30,000 ft)
- Carrying a payload of 5,000 kg (11,000 lb) at 1,000 km/h (337 mph).

Additionally, the Y1B-17A's new service ceiling was higher, 12,000 meters (38,000 ft), compared to the Y1B-17's 9,327 meters (30,600 ft).

Originally built to ground test the airframe's endurance, this was actually the 14th Y1B-17 built (37-369), which Boeing upgraded with General Electric exhaust-driven turbochargers and designated the Y1B-17A.
Designed by Sanford Moss, the engine's exhaust turned the turbine's steel-alloy blades, forcing high-pressure air into the compressor of the Wright Cyclone GR-1820-39 engine.

Scheduled to fly in 1937, it encountered problems with the turbochargers and its first flight was delayed until April 29, 1938. The aircraft was delivered to the Army on January 31, 1939.

B-17B

First production model ordered in 39 units.
Compared to the Y1B-17 it had larger rudder and flaps.
The small turret in the upper part of the nose was replaced by a
12.7 mm swiveling machine gun, the front part was redesigned
with the introduction of a glass nose consisting of 10 framed
windows.

B-17Bs at March Field, California, prior to the attack on Pearl Harbor.

Of the 39 aircraft of this type, 19 were later modified and
converted to C/D with the nose and frontal armament of the E
version. The Wright R-1820-51 engines provided 1,200 hp at
take-off.

B-17C

Ordered in 38 units.

Twin 12.7 mm machine guns were installed in the dorsal and (redesigned) ventral positions and single weapons of the same caliber were in the lateral positions, now without the transparent bubble cover, while two mounts on the sides of the nose replaced the single, central, for 7.62 mm weapons.

B-17C 40-2065 - 8 November 1941 North Africa.

Also featured were self-sealing tanks and armor for the crew.
- The engines were Wright R-1820-65 Cyclones with turbocharger, 1,200 hp at 7,620 meters and 91 octane fuel.

Of the 39 produced, 20 were sold to Great Britain, which used them as Fortress Mk I; these aircraft did not make a good impression: after three months of use, 10 aircraft had been lost,

half of them in accidents. The machine guns tended to jam due to ice at high altitudes and the bombings proved very inaccurate. The only difference with the American model was the different machine gun in the nose and a different refueling system.
The Americans did not consider the B-17C ready for combat but the British were so desperate at the time that they used it immediately, not without problems.

B-17D

Externally similar to the B-17C, the version introduced numerous modifications.
The engine flaps were modified to improve cooling, the external bomb hooks were eliminated, the electrical system was revised and a new element was added to the crew.

B-17D captured by the Japanese Army.

The defensive armament was also revised, bringing it to 7 machine guns, including a light 7.62 mm caliber and 6 heavy 12.7 mm.
 • 42 B-17Ds were built and another 18 were obtained from the conversion of B-17Cs.

The crew was 10 men.

First version produced in large quantities (512 units). Three hundred additional B-17Es, ordered at a later time, were then completed in the "F" version.

- The version of the B-17E sold to the British, 45 units, was renamed Fortress IIA and was used for hunting submarines in the Atlantic.

The "E" was the first version of the bomber with a servo-assisted turret and a defensive position at the rear; it was now evident, in fact, that the B17 "C" and "D" lacked ballistic armament in the rear area.

B-17E.

The main British bombers and the B-24 Liberator already had tail gunners from their conception, with powered turrets on the British aircraft.

Boeing, rather than design a new aircraft, chose to develop the excellent airframe of the Model 299, practically rebuilding the B-17 from behind the wing to the extreme aft. Due to the tapered design of the aircraft, it was not possible to install a powered turret in the tail, but a manually controlled twin position was embarked.

A new and large vertical fin was adopted, derived from that of the Model 307 "Starliner", a civil development of the Model 299 of which it maintained the same wing platform and the same engines.

The rear tail wheel became completely retractable.

- The tail guns were controlled by means of levers and transmissions; the gunner operated them sitting behind an armored glass, with an aiming system integral with the levers themselves. The firing sector was limited to 30° both in the horizontal and vertical planes.
- The lateral positions in the center of the fuselage were replaced by open doors, from which, however, the wind could enter inside.
- For the dorsal defense, a Sperry dorsal turret was installed behind the pilot's seat, in the position already used in the "D" version.
- The ventral defense included a new remote-controlled Bendix twin turret, operated by a gunner in a prone position using a periscope aiming system. Difficult to use, being a source of dizziness and other discomfort for the gunner, it was only used temporarily. The protection of the ventral sector was improved after the first 113 examples with the introduction of a new spherical turret produced by Sperry.

In total, eight 12.7 mm Browning machine guns were initially installed, weapons with excellent mechanical and ballistic characteristics.

The ball turret had the weapons fixed to the structure which, in turn, was designed to rotate on its axes both for aiming and to allow access to the gunner inside. The gunner sat on the hatch in a narrow and uncomfortable position that required the use of small-built personnel.

The Sperry turret was, however, very satisfactory as it allowed to cover the entire lower sector without dead spots.

- The maximum speed and the cruising speed, compared to the previous version, were reduced by 10 km/h. The rate of climb increased as a result of the increase in maximum take-off weight of about 50%, an element destined, however, to grow further with the embarkation of additional weapons, components and electronic equipment.

A prototype was derived from the B-17E with the Allison V-1710-89 engines, a 1,420 hp water-cooled V12 engine built by the Vega division of the Lockheed Corporation and designated with the acronym Vega XB-38. A real comparison with the B-17E was never made and since the Allison engine was needed in the equipment of other aircraft the project was abandoned.

B-17F

The "F" version incorporated about 400 modifications compared to the B-17E from which it differed externally only for the nose completely in plexiglass without a frame except for an optically flat sector for aiming the bombs.
3,405 examples were built, of which 2,300 by Boeing, 605 by Douglas and 500 by Lockheed Vega; 19 were sold by Great Britain.
The most important modifications were the new version of the Wright R-1820-97 engines with 1,350 hp at altitude, 1,200 hp at take-off and 1,000 hp at 7,620 meters and 2,300 rpm.

B-17F.

The version of the B-17F used by the British to patrol the English Channel was renamed Fortress II.
The engines were equipped with a General Electric GE B-22 turbo-compressor and Hamilton Standard propellers with "paddle" blades of 3.53 meters in diameter, 14 cm more than the previous ones.
The "feathering" of the new blades required a different profile of the engine fairing.

The new engines allowed the operating ceiling to be increased to 11,580 meters and the maximum speed to 515 km/h; subsequent increases in weight (4,500 kg) introduced following further improvements, reduced the maximum speed to 481 km/h, with the use of emergency power.

- Other improvements involved the landing gear, brakes, oxygen distribution system, bomb racks, spherical turret and oil tanks, which also became self-sealing.

The major problem faced by the B-17F in its European theater service was its forward firepower, and several improvements were studied to increase it.

Among the modifications requested in Europe was the addition of more machine guns to the bow, in spherical "pocket" mounts in the plexiglass profile, bringing the maximum number of weapons on board to 12-13.

However, the spherical "pocket" mounts at the bow were not adequate for firing at 0° bearing.

So side-by-side weapons on a single support frame were tested (however, the recoil was too high) and side guns with a front faceplate similar to the emplacements of the later B-17Gs.

The final solution was a single 12.7 mm machine gun installed in a triangular recess at the end of the glass nose.

- Another notable change was the installation of two additional 270-gallon (1,022-liter) gasoline tanks in each outer wing, increasing the total fuel capacity from 1,730 to 2,810 gallons (6,550 to 10,638 liters).
- Range increased from 1,300 to 2,200 miles (2,090 to 3,540 km), which provided an additional three hours of flight time, but at the same time required 38 minutes to reach 20,000 feet (6,100 m), compared to the 25 minutes required by the earlier B-17Fs.

Further modifications were necessary to vent gasoline vapor from the outer wings, which had always been a primary source of fires and explosions during flight.

The next improvement to the aircraft saw the installation of remotely controlled Bendix turrets positioned under the nose.

B-17G

It was the most representative version of the entire series.
It was built in 8,680 units, of which:
- 4,035 units produced by Boeing.
- 2,250 by Lockheed-Vega.
- 2,395 by Douglas.

The 85 B-17Gs sold to the British were renamed Fortress III.
Three of these aircraft were transferred to Coastal Command in the Azores and equipped with radar for weather reconnaissance.
The RAF B-17s were used mainly in the 100th Group, starting in February 1944, equipped with electronic countermeasures equipment to confuse German radars.
- Forty units went to the U.S. Navy for anti-submarine (PB-1G) and weather reconnaissance (PB-1W) duties. The "G" variant could be considered a production development of the "F" version and, in the opinion of the pilots, it was simply an "F" with a forward turret.

As a result of the aerodynamic resistance caused by the new armament, performance was further reduced, with the maximum speed dropped to 486 km/h, even if the operational speed achievable corresponded to the more likely value of 446 km/h. Initially the machines were delivered without the bow side machine guns, which were embarked first by the departments and then directly on the production lines.
Due to the large space occupied by the forward turret control devices, on the "G" version the aiming sight was suspended inside the plexiglass forward end of the aircraft. In the winter of 1933-44, the Sperry dorsal turret was replaced by a similar turret produced by Bendix, less aerodynamically profiled, but which allowed for better visibility and greater speed in responding to electromechanical controls.
To improve the maneuverability of the weapons in the center of the fuselage and to give more space to the gunners who were in each other's way in the narrow tail, the right station was

positioned further forward than the left. In addition, the stations, initially open when the weapons were used - exposing the gunners to the rigors of high altitude - were equipped with plexiglass covers in early 1944.

B17G: view from the bomber's position; in the center, the Norden aiming system.

An opening was made in the ceiling of the radio compartment from which it was possible to operate an additional dorsal machine gun. However, this installation was often eliminated in the operational area because the weapon's firing range was rather limited and, especially towards the end of the war, the threat from German fighters was now reduced.

- More important was the modification of the tail position in order to improve its limited firing sector. A "reflection" type collimator was installed and the windowed surface was increased, thus widening the firing range.

  The weapons were enclosed in a hemispherical dome and moved closer to the gunner; the regulation mechanism of the turbo-compressor was also modified with an electric drive, rather than a hydraulic one which was difficult to use.

Another important modification was the installation of the B-22 turbo-compressor with a higher speed turbine and better performance at altitude.

YB-40

The YB-40 prototype was built by Lockheed-Vega by converting the second B-17-BO, significantly increasing its firepower. A pair of machine guns were installed in each lateral position, a second dorsal turret in the radio compartment and an additional turret developed by Bendix operated by a gunner sitting in the bombardier's position.

The aircraft therefore had 14 12.7 mm guns, in practice one or two more than many "F"s operational in England and modified on the field, all this however in the face of a strong increase in maximum take-off weight, also due to the 11,000 rounds of ammunition (three times those of the B-17F), which could be increased to more than 17,000 with an additional provision in the bomb bay.

The variant was approved in the winter of 1942-43, and an order for 12 YB-40s followed. The armament was increased to 16 12.7 mm guns with two more lateral ones at the bow.

On these aircraft, assigned to the 327th B.S., the particular weight distribution moved the center of gravity back considerably, creating no small difficulty in maintaining the formation with the "F"s once the war load was released.

The variant was not a success at all and only 11 more aircraft were ordered (and seven completed) before abandoning production.

One B-17F was taken over by the US Navy for evaluation in the patrol role.

After the war, 48 B-17G-BO and -VE were purchased by the US Navy, and of these, 31 were used for advanced electronic reconnaissance, designated PB-1W by the US Navy. A characteristic feature of these conversions was the installation of an APS-20 search radar in a large radome under the central part of the fuselage. The remaining machines, designated PB-1G, went to the US Coast Guard, and some were modified to carry a lifeboat, also carrying a naval search radar on the bow.

Similar to the B-17H, the PB-1G were also known as Jumbo. In particular, they were used for long-range weather reconnaissance and for finding and tracking icebergs.

Designation that identified, in the immediate post-war period, two B-17Gs used for flight testing of new engines; in this context, the cockpit was moved back towards the center of the fuselage.

One of the two aircraft was taken over by Curtiss-Wright to evaluate in flight a Wright XT-35 turboprop engine installed in the bow. This engine delivered 5,500 hp, proving by itself more powerful than the 4 piston engines. Later, the same aircraft embarked the XJ-65 turbojet, positioned under the forward section of the fuselage.

A second B-17G was used by Pratt & Whitney for testing the XT-34 turboprop engine; finally, at the beginning of the 1950s, a third B-17G was used for experiments related to the Allison T-56 turboprop, installed in the bow without moving the cockpit back.

BQ-7 Aphrodite

Towards the end of the war, a number of B-17s (probably 25) were modified for Operation Aphrodite.
- The objective was to destroy U-boat bases, V-1 launch pads and other heavily fortified installations.

The planes were equipped with remote control systems and loaded with 9,000 kg of high explosives. They were to be flown by two-man crew (volunteers) who took off, aimed the plane at the target and bailed out by parachute after passing control of the plane to another B-17 who would control it remotely.
It didn't work: none of the 15 BQ-7s used hit the target, one crashed in Great Britain leaving a crater 100 metres in diameter and several men died from various problems in the parachute jump.

Crew

The crew of a B-17 consisted of 10 people:
- Pilot
- Co-pilot
- Bombardier/Right front gunner
- Navigator/Left front gunner
- Upper gunner
- Radio operator
- Right side gunner
- Left side gunner
- Ventral gunner
- Tail gunner.

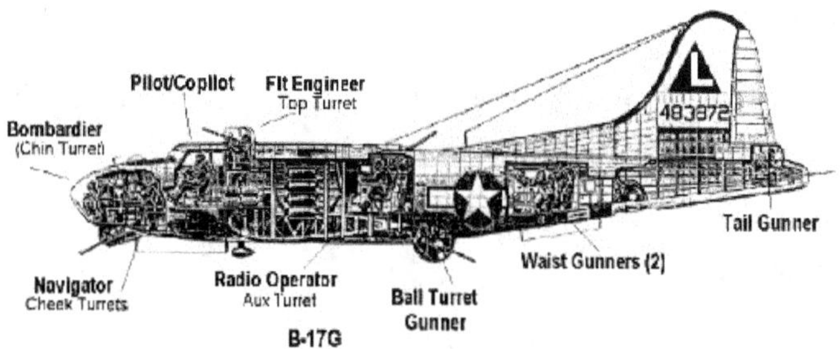

Technical Features

Dimensions and weights

- Length: 22.66 meters
- Wingspan: 31.62 meters
- Height: 5.82 meters
- Wing area: 131.92 m2
- Empty weight: 16,391 kg
- Loaded weight: 24,495 kg
- Maximum take-off weight: 29,710 kg
- Landing gear: semi-retractable in the fuselage, automatic
- Fuel capacity: 10,637 liters + 3,104 liters in an internal auxiliary tank

Propulsion

- Engine: 4 Wright R-1820-97 "Cyclone" radial engines with turbocharger
- Power: 1,200 hp (895 kW) each

Performance

- Maximum speed: 462 km/h
- Cruise speed: 293 km/h
- Rate of climb: 4.6 m/sec
- Range: 5,500 km
- Ceiling: 10,850 meters

Armament

Machine guns: 13 Browning M2 caliber 50 BMG (12.7 mm):
- 2 in the front defensive position, under the transparent nose, 12.7 mm, with 300 rounds each.
- 2 in the front lateral defensive positions 12.7 mm, with 500 rounds each.

- 2 in the dorsal defensive position "Martin" 12.7 mm, with 200 rounds each.
- 1 in the radio operator's position, with 500 rounds.
- 2 in the ventral defensive position "Sperry" 12.7 mm, with 340 rounds each.
- 2 in the caudal defensive position 12.7 mm, with 500 rounds each.
- 2 in the sides of the nose 12.7 mm

Bombs: 7,983 kg of bombs in total:
- 8 bombs of 454 kg
- 6 bombs of 726 kg
- 16 bombs of 227 kg
- 2 bombs of 1,814 kg

Cost

The cost of a B-17G produced in the years 1943-44 was:
- Fuselage: $127,069
- Engines: $38,483
- Propellers: $11,900
- Electrical system: $9,040
- Armament: $6,342
- Miscellaneous equipment: $45,495
- Total: $238,329

Figures

- 640,036 tons of bombs dropped by the B-17s on European targets.
- 12,731 units produced.
- 4,750 B-17s lost in combat (1 shot down for every 3 produced).
- 20,000 German aircraft reported shot down by its machine guns (23 enemy aircraft shot down for every 1,000 missions).
- 250,000 American airmen flew the B-17.
- 45,000 airmen died.

Famous B-17 Pilots and Crew Members

Many B-17 crew members have been decorated for valor, and 17 have received the Medal of Honor, the highest military decoration awarded by the United States.
The Medal of Honor, established on July 12, 1862, is the highest military decoration awarded by the United States Government, similar to the British Victoria Cross, the French Legion of Honor, or the Italian Medaglia d'oro al valor militare.
The Medal of Honor is often awarded personally to the recipient or, in the case of posthumous decoration, to the family members, by the President of the United States; because of its high value, the medal is specially protected by U.S. law. Because of its nature, the medal is frequently awarded posthumously.

It is sometimes referred to as the "Congressional Medal of Honor", as the President of the United States presents the decoration "in the name of Congress". It is awarded to a member of the United States Armed Forces who has demonstrated: "an act of courage and intrepidity at the risk of his life above and beyond the call of duty while engaged in combat with an enemy of the United States."

Members of all branches of the U.S. Armed Forces are eligible to receive the medal. There are three different designs of the award, depending on the armed forces to which the decorated individual belongs; the Army and Air Force each have their own versions, while the Navy, Marine Corps, and Coast Guard all share the same design. The Medal of Honor is one of only two military awards to be worn around the neck presented by the United States Armed Forces and is the only one awarded to members of the U.S. Armed Forces. The other is the Legion of Merit at the rank of commander, and it is authorized to be applied for only by foreign dignitaries generally of the rank of Chiefs of Staff.

A total of 3,464 medals have been awarded to 3,445 individuals, with 19 individuals receiving two medals. Of the latter, 14 received two medals for two separate actions and five were decorated with both the Navy and Army medals for the same action.

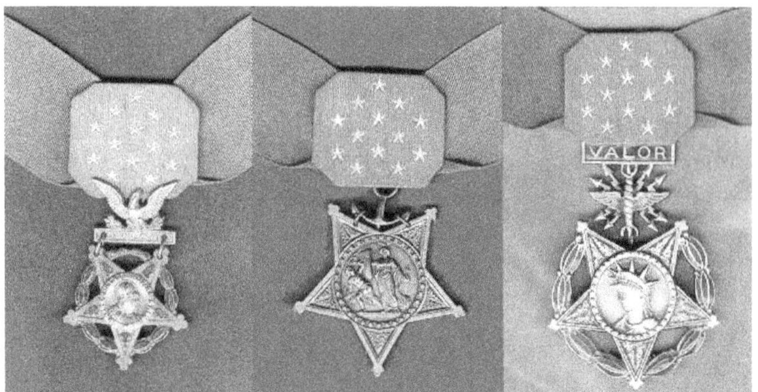

From left: Medal of Honor Army, Navy/Marine Corps/Coast Guard, Air Force.

- Brigadier Generale Frederick Walker Castle (in memory).

Commander of the 487th Bomb Group, on his thirtieth mission, he remained at the controls of his stricken B-17 to allow the crew to bail out on December 24, 1944. Frederick W. Castle was buried at the Henri-Chapelle American Cemetery, Liège Province, Belgium; he was awarded the Medal of Honor, the highest military decoration awarded by the President of the United States, for personal acts of valor above and beyond the call of duty.

- 2nd Lt Robert Edward Femoyer (in memory)

The B-17 Navigator was hit by three bullets during a raid. He refused morphine to stay lucid and continue his task and, despite excruciating pain, managed to give directions for the return route for two and a half hours, during which he made his isolated bomber make six changes of course to avoid concentrations of enemy aircraft. Only after arriving safely over the English Channel did he accept the painkiller, but died thirty minutes after landing from the wounds he had suffered.

- 1st Lt Donald Gott e 2nd Lt William E. Metzger, Jr. (both in memory)

Pilot and co-pilot of a B-17, during a bombing mission their plane was hit by anti-aircraft fire.
Three of the four engines were knocked out and several crew members were injured. Among them, the radio operator with an amputated arm would not survive the parachute jump. To save his crew, Gott, despite his desperate condition, decided to attempt a return to Allied territory and an emergency landing. Once in friendly territory, the rest of the crew parachuted to safety, while Metzger decided to stay on board to help his commander.
Just before touching down, the plane exploded in flight, killing the two and the injured radio operator.

- 2nd Lt David Kingsley (in memory)

B-17 Aimer, after completing the mission, his plane was hit by three Messerschmitt Bf 109s.
He went first to the tail gunner and then to the dorsal gunner to treat both of their wounds. Immediately afterward, the plane's commander gave the order to bail out due to the imminent risk of explosion.
Kingsley assisted the tail gunner and when he realized that the tail gunner's parachute was missing, he gave him his own. He was last seen by his fellow crew members bailing out, standing on the bomb bay walkway. The abandoned plane crashed shortly after, killing him. His body was found in the wreckage and buried in Arlington National Cemetery.

- 1st Lt William R. Lawley, Jr.

A B-17 pilot, he was wounded in the face during a mission in which eight crew members were wounded and the co-pilot was killed. Able to fly with only one hand, he gave the order to abandon the plane, but was told that two of the crew members could not do so. He then decided to try to save them by returning to Allied territory, despite the damage to the engines and the load of bombs still on board. Unconscious from the effort and loss of blood, he was revived by the gunner and eventually managed to avoid attacks by enemy fighters and keep the plane in the air until landing at a small fighter base in England.

- 1st Lt Walter E. Truemper e Sgt Archibald Mathies (both in memory)

Navigator and gunner of B-17, they refused to abandon the plane where they were flying and that had been hit leaving the pilot unconscious and the co-pilot dead. They decided to take the controls and managed to return to England where they had all the other crew members parachuted. It was deemed impossible for untrained pilots to land such a damaged plane, but they refused to abandon the pilot who was still alive. On the third attempt to land, the plane crashed to the ground killing the three on board.

- 1st Lt Jack Mathis (in memory)

B-17 Aimer was tasked with indicating the target to the rest of the formation with his launch.
During the approach, he was hit by flak so hard that he was thrown backwards into the next compartment. Although terribly wounded, he returned to his aiming position and correctly indicated the target before dying at his post.

- 1st Lt Edward Michael

B-17 pilot, after realizing that his aimer could not abandon the plane due to damage to the parachute, decided despite his serious injuries to save him by attempting to return to England even with the plane severely damaged and pursued by enemy fighters. Despite fires on board, extensive damage to the plane that remained with the bomb bay open, landing gear, flaps and instruments inoperative, he managed to land.

- 1st Lt John C. Morgan

B-17 co-pilot found himself during a mission struggling with his fellow pilot who was shot in the head and who, in a confused state, was trying to regain control but was unable to fly the plane. Even with the crew wounded or stunned by anoxia, he decided to stay in formation and continue the mission, flying with one hand and struggling with the other for over two hours.

- Capt Harl Pease (in memory)

A B-17 pilot in the Asian theater, in order to participate in an attack, he chose the least damaged aircraft from a group of planes declared unfit for flight and joined the others for the mission. Even with the plane in precarious conditions, he managed to remain with the formation and hit the target. Attacked by many Japanese planes, he crashed after a fierce fight. It was later discovered that, having been taken prisoner by the Japanese, he was subjected to mistreatment and beheaded along with other prisoners of war.

- Brig Gen Kenneth Walker

For remarkable leadership skills beyond the call of duty, involving personal valor and daring at the extreme risk of his life. In command of the 5th Bomber Command, he repeatedly accompanied his units on deep-bombing missions into enemy territory, developing a remarkably effective bombing technique in the presence of heavy opposition.
On 5 January 1943 he directed a daylight bombing attack against ships in the port of Rabaul, in the presence of heavy air and ground opposition, scoring hits on nine enemy ships. During the action his aircraft was heavily damaged by enemy fighter fire.

- Maj Jay Zeamer, Jr.

A B-17 pilot in the South Pacific theater, he volunteered for a photo-reconnaissance mission over the heavily defended Buka area (Solomon Islands). During the recovery over Buka airfield, the crew observed about twenty enemy fighters take off, but Commander Zeamer continued his mission, even under attack from Japanese forces. Wounded in both arms and legs, he continued to maneuver his plane, allowing the gunners to sustain a 40-minute fight, in which five enemy fighters were shot down. He handed over the controls to the co-pilot only at the end of the fight, but continued to exercise command until landing.

- Capitano Werner G. Goering

American-born grandson of the famous Luftwaffe commander during World War II, Hermann Göring.

- Immanuel J. Klette (1918–1988)

German-American of the second generation whose 91 combat missions set the record for missions flown by an Eighth Air Force pilot in World War II.

- Col Frank Kurtz (1911–1996)

Most decorated USAAF pilot of World War II; commander of the 463rd Bombardment Group (Heavy), 15th Air Force, Celone Field, Foggia; survivor of the attack on Clark Field in the Philippines; bronze medalist in diving at the 1932 Olympics; father of actress Swoosie Kurtz.

- Lt Col Nancy Love (1914–1976) and Betty Gillies (1908–1998)

The first women certified to fly the B-17, in 1943.

- Col Robert K. Morgan (1918–2004)

Memphis Belle Pilot.

- Lt Col Robert Rosenthal (1917–2007)

Commander of the only B-17, "Rosie's Riveters", that survived an 8th Air Force 100th Bomb Group raid on Münster in 1943, he was decorated with sixteen medals (including one from the United Kingdom and one from France), and led the raid on Berlin on 3 February 1945 that probably killed Roland Freisler, the Third Reich's infamous "hanging judge".

- Brig Gen Paul Tibbets (1915–2007)

He flew with the 97th Bombardment Group (Heavy) with both the 8th Air Force in England and the 12th Air Force in North Africa; later becoming famous as the pilot of the B-29 Enola Gay that dropped the atomic bomb on Hiroshima, Japan.

Memphis Belle

The Flying Fortress Memphis Belle was one of 12,750 B-17s built by Boeing. The aircraft is a B-17F-10-BO (serial number 41-24485) built in July 1942 by Boeing that served for seven months, from November 7, 1942 to May 17, 1943, completing 25 missions in the 324th Bomb Squadron, part of the 91st Bomb Group, Eighth Air Force, based in Bassingbourne, England, without losing a single crew member and without ever suffering serious damage. For this reason, it became the most famous bomber in the US Air Force.
The aircraft was named "Memphis Belle" by the commander pilot Col. Robert Morgan, in honor of his beautiful fiancée Miss Margaret Polk. The nose of the aircraft was painted by Corporal Tony Starcer inspired by the famous pin-ups drawn by the famous artist of the time George Petty, a student of the even more famous Alberto Vargas.

- The general command of the American Air Force had established a maximum of 25 missions as an incentive for the crews to return home; in fact, morale was low since more than 80% of the bombers had been shot down during the first three months of the war in the skies of Europe.

Also for this reason the Memphis Belle became an example to follow. During the 25 missions it flew 148 hours, 50 minutes and traveled more than 20,000 miles, unloading about 60 tons of bombs.
Due to the damage suffered in combat, almost every part of the plane was replaced at least once.
The 26th mission of the Memphis Belle, the most important for the American Government, was to return to the United States and begin a promotional tour of the Air Force as a thank you to the American population, who were making considerable efforts due to the war.
The crew members visited over 32 cities where they received a welcome as heroes.

Their mascot, the dog named "stuka" traveled with them across the Atlantic, even taking part in the final thank you flight. The aircraft is a B-17F-10-BO (serial number 41-24485) built in July 1942 by Boeing that served for seven months, from 7 November 1942 to 17 May 1943, flying 25 missions in the 324th Bomb Squadron, part of the 91st Bomb Group, Eighth Air Force, based at Bassingbourne, England.

In 1944, a documentary called The Memphis Belle: A Story of a Flying Fortress was made by filmmaker William Wyler to tell the story of the bomber's twenty-fifth mission. In 2001, the Library of Congress declared the film "culturally significant" and selected it for preservation in the National Film Registry. On May 17, 1987, exactly 44 years after it flew its 25th mission, a museum was dedicated to the Memphis Belle, and over 25,000 people attended the opening. A formation of B-17s flew over the site, scattering thousands of rose petals, and Miss Polk and the crew warmly thanked the audience.

The crew of the Memphis Belle consisted of:
- Pilot: Captain Robert Morgan
- Co-Pilot: Captain James A. Verinis
- Bombardier (and right front gunner): Captain Vincent B. Evans

- Navigator (and left front gunner): Captain Charles B. Leighton
- Radio Operator: Sergeant Robert J. Hanson
- Engineer and Upper Turret Gunner: Sergeant Harold P. Loch, Sergeant Leviticus Dillon, Sergeant Eugene Adkins
- Left Side Gunner: Sergeant Clarence E. Winchell
- Left Side Gunner: Sergeant E. Scott Miller, Sergeant Casimer A. Nastal
- Tail Gunner: Sergeant John P. Quinlan
- Belly Gunner: Cecil H. Scott

The Crew of the Memphis Belle.

On May 13, 1943, co-pilot Jim Verinis became the first member of the crew to complete his 25-mission tour.

Pilot Robert Morgan and most of the rest of the crew completed their tour on May 17. The next day, the aircraft flew its 25th and final mission.

The following is a list of missions flown by Belle during World War II:

1. November 7, 1942 - Brest, France

2. November 9, 1942 - St. Nazaire, France
3. November 17, 1942 - St. Nazaire, France
4. December 6, 1942 - Lille, France
5. December 20, 1942 - Romilly-sur-Seine, France
6. January 3, 1943 - St. Nazaire, France
7. January 13, 1943 - Lille, France
8. January 23, 1943 - Lorient, France
9. February 4, 1943 - Emden, Germany
10. February 14, 1943 - Hamm, Germany
11. February 16, 1943 - St. Nazaire, France
12. February 26, 1943 - Wilhelmshaven, Germany
13. February 27, 1943 - Brest, France
14. March 6, 1943 - Lorient, France
15. March 12, 1943 - Rouen, France
16. March 13, 1943 - Abbeville, France
17. March 22, 1943 - Wilhelmshaven, Germany
18. March 28, 1943 - Rouen, France
19. April 5, 1943 - Antwerp, Belgium
20. April 16, 1943 - Lorient, France
21. April 17, 1943 - Bremen (city), Germany
22. May 1, 1943 - St. Nazaire, France
23. May 4, 1943 - Antwerp, Belgium
24. May 15, 1943 - Wilhelmshaven, Germany
25. May 17, 1943 - Lorient, France

Completed the cycle of missions the Memphis Belle returned to the United States where it was used for propaganda purposes and to advertise the war loan.

After the war the Belle would have suffered the same fate as all the old bombers but a providential intervention by the mayor of Memphis saved the plane from dismantling for the modest sum of $ 350.

The plane was parked outdoors as a static model until the 1980s, deteriorating due to the weather conditions and repeated vandalism.

Original Memphis Belle, pictured in flight on June 9, 1943.

Under pressure from the newly formed Memphis Belle Memorial Association (MBMA), an attempt was made to find a better home for the aircraft, which had returned to the ownership of the Air Force in the 1970s. The aircraft was then moved near the Mississippi River, where an area was set up with a roof that, however, did not protect the Belle from the elements. In October 2003, the aircraft was moved to Millington to be reconditioned, but in September 2004, tired of the city's continued delays in preserving the historic B-17, the National Museum of the United States Air Force admitted that it wanted to regain possession of the aircraft in order to repair it and subsequently display it in the museum in Dayton (Ohio). On August 30, 2005, the MBMA declared that it was unable to repair the Belle due to lack of funds and agreed to the Air Force's demands on the condition that it could make a final public display at Millington, Tennessee from September 30 to October 2, 2005. The B-17 then arrived in Dayton, Ohio in mid-October 2005.

The original Memphis Belle was no longer in a flying condition, so a B-17G-85-DL, (serial number 44-83546, registered N3703G) was converted to a B-17F and painted like the Belle for use in the filming of the 1990 movie and for display at various air shows as a flying example.

Historically, however, it appears that the first B-17 to complete 25 missions was "Hell's Angels", serial number 41-24577 on 13 May 1943 belonging to the 358th Bombardment Squadron RAF Molesworth.

The "Memphis Belle" was the first to complete 25 missions and return to the United States, while Hell's Angels continued to fly until 13 December 1943, when it completed 48 combat missions and was withdrawn from combat.

- Colonel Robert Morgan, pilot of the Memphis Belle, died May 16, 2004, in an Ashville, North Carolina, hospital from a broken neck he suffered three weeks earlier in a fall after attending an air show. He was 85.

Il B-17 Hell's Angels e il suo equipaggio

A page of history

In the early spring of 1943, an Allied P-38, running low on fuel, attempted an emergency landing near the coast of Sardinia.
The pilot, however, was taken prisoner by the Italians before he had a chance to destroy his plane.
An Italian pilot, Second Lieutenant Guido Rossi, suggested using the captured (and still operational) P-38 against the American bombers: the strategy was to wait until the bombing began, take off, and attack by surprise.
n the following weeks, a fair number of American bombers (mostly B-17s) were shot down with this simple system. Believing they were near an Allied P-38, and reassured by radio contact (Rossi spoke fluent English), no one in the B-17s was concerned about its approach.
Once at close range, Guido Rossi opened fire and quickly shot down the bomber. In the hierarchy of the Allied forces, no one was too concerned about the downed bombers, it was normal for some planes to leave and never return; after all, in the Anglo-American war language the term used to indicate losses, deaths, downings, is casualties (literally: "coincidence"). Rossi's operations on this P-38 continued for several weeks, until June 4, 1943. That day, at the height of the island of Pantelleria, a B-17 was preparing to bomb, when it noticed a P-38 approaching. Having recognized it by its shape, they thought it was Allied forces, and began to drop their bombs as expected.
But before they could realize what was happening, the P-38 opened fire and shot down the B-17. The story of the "ghost" P-38 takes a turn here because for the first time there was a survivor, the pilot of the downed B-17,
Second Lieutenant Harold Fisher, whom the Americans managed to save. At first, when Fisher said he had been hit by an allied P-38, they did not believe him.
Once the leaders were convinced, and thinking that it was a lone P-38 always in flight, Fisher proposed and obtained to fly a modified B-17 (with more weapons to withstand the aerial confrontation) in order to intercept the "ghost" P-38.

Since after several flights he still had not managed to meet it, it was decided that it was time to abandon the project.

But American intelligence had in the meantime managed to discover the secret of Pulcinella, that is, the identity of Guido Rossi and his wife Gina. They had Gina's face drawn on the nose of a B-17 as a provocation, a B-17 that took off on August 31, 1943, along with other planes to bomb Pisa. The B-17 in question was piloted by Fisher. After the bombing of Pisa - from which it suffered several damages due to the Italian counterattack - the bomber team noticed a P-38 approaching.

Guido Rossi, as always, contacted Fisher by radio; at first Fisher was not sure if it was Rossi and provoked him by talking to him about Gina. This, even more than having noticed Gina's face roughly drawn on the nose of the B-17, made Rossi nervous, who immediately attacked.

Fisher ordered his men on board to fire on the P-38, managing to damage it; Rossi attempted to destroy the B-17 by trying to shoot down his P-38 on top of it, but the fighter could no longer hold the flight and was therefore forced to ditch.

Guido Rossi was taken prisoner, and Fisher was awarded a medal. Fisher died shortly after the end of the war, in a plane crash. And at his funeral, among the others, there was Guido Rossi himself in mourning..

Eighth Air Force

The Eighth Air Force (8th Air Force, 8th AF) is a numbered air force of the United States Air Force. Its main command is at Barksdale Air Force Base (Louisiana). This air force is historically derived from the almost legendary Eighth Air Force (nicknamed The Mighty Eighth for its power and determination) of World War II, which controlled and directed throughout the conflict in Europe the strategic bombing campaign conducted with increasing success by the famous American four-engined B-17 Flying Fortress heavy bombers from bases in the United Kingdom.

After being formed in January 1942, the Eighth Air Force, consisting mainly of VIII Bomber Command and VIII Fighter Command, continued for two years its daytime bombing raids in large high-altitude formations against industrial and military targets in Europe and occupied Germany.

In February 1944, the U.S. Air Force was reorganized, with the original Eighth Air Force headquarters being used to form the centralized command of the United States Strategic Command in Europe, and the VIII Bomber Command headquarters becoming the command of the original Eighth Air Force's bomber and fighter units and continuing strategic missions until the end of the war.

- The Eighth Air Force was a key component of SAC's strategic nuclear strike forces throughout the Cold War, with units also participating in the Korean War and the Vietnam War.

The Eighth Air Force is currently under the command of Air Forces Strategic - Global Strike, which is the primary air component of the United States Strategic Command (USSTRATCOM), the joint command responsible for leading strategic bomber and ballistic missile units capable of launching a nuclear strike.

The history of the Eighth Air Force officially began on January 2, 1942, when it was activated at Savannah Air Force Base,

Georgia, as part of the grandiose program to strengthen the United States Army Air Force, planned by President Franklin D. Roosevelt at the beginning of the United States' participation in World War II. In short order, on January 5, 1942, General Carl Spaatz assumed command of the new air formation with headquarters at Bolling Field, Washington, DC. The Eighth Air Force was designated to constitute the American air component to be sent as soon as possible to Europe to participate in the war against Nazi Germany, and on January 8, 1942, the formation of the "U.S. Armed Forces in the British Isles" (USAFBI) under the command of General James Eugene Chaney was publicly announced, while on May 12, 1942, the first contingent of the Eighth Air Force arrived in England. On 15 June 1942, General Spaatz arrived in the United Kingdom, established a new headquarters, and on 18 June 1942 took over command of the Eighth Air Force at Bushy Park, fifteen kilometres southwest of London.

The Eighth Air Force controlled a number of operational components under its direct command:

- VIII Bomber Command, established on 19 January 1942, responsible for strategic bombing using four-engined heavy bombers.
- VIII Fighter Command, established on 19 January 1942, responsible for fighter escort missions for heavy bombers.
- VIII Air Support Command, established on 24 April 1942, responsible for aerial reconnaissance, troop transport, and tactical bombing using twin-engined medium bombers.
- VIII Air Service Command, later renamed VIII Air Force Service Command, responsible for logistical support.

The most important component of the Eighth Air Force was certainly the VIII Bomber Command which was initially activated at Langley Field, Virginia, and was transferred on 10 February 1942 to Savannah Air Force Base, Georgia..

Brigadier General Ira C. Eaker took command of the formations of VIII Bomber Command with the task of directing the independent strategic air campaign of the American air forces, he organized his headquarters next to that of the British Bomber

Command at Daws Hill where an advanced detachment arrived on 23 February 1942 in advance of the first organic air units; the advanced echelon of the 97th Bombardment Group arrived in the United Kingdom on 9 June 1942, while the first Boeing B-17 Flying Fortress heavy bomber landed at Prestwick on 1 July 1942. The strategic planning of the American high command was extremely ambitious and envisaged an impressive increase in the forces available to the Eighth Air Force which would be accompanied by a massive logistical effort supported by the collaboration of the British authorities which included the use of existing structures and the construction of almost a hundred new installations and airfields.

Original plans called for the Eighth Air Force to have 1,000 aircraft by August 1942, rising to 3,500 by April 1943; detailed plans called for the initial establishment of 66 air groups with 700 heavy bombers, 342 medium bombers, and 960 fighters.

These projects were too ambitious and the effective groups had to be immediately reduced to 54, while the 137 groups planned for 1943 were completed only in June 1944.

The transfer of aircraft assigned to the Eighth Air Force took place by air via the Maine-Goose Bay-Greenland-Iceland-Scotland route and, after the first bomber arrived on July 1, 1942, continued regularly over the months: by the end of August, 386 aircraft had arrived, including 119 B-17s, to which another 700 aircraft were added by the end of the year.

Despite the diversion of many groups to the Mediterranean front to reinforce the Twelfth Air Force, charged with supporting Operation Torch, the Eighth Air Force had 668 aircraft at its disposal at the end of 1942, including 338 four-engine heavy bombers.

At the end of the year, due to the opening of the North African front, the command structure of the Eighth Air Force also changed; General Carl Spaatz moved to General Dwight Eisenhower as the senior commander of the Allied Air Forces in North Africa, which in February 1943 became the Northwest African Air Force, while General Ira Eaker, already commander of the VIII Bomber Command, assumed the senior command of the Eighth Air Force in Great Britain on 1 December 1942; finally, General Newton Longfellow became the commander of the VIII Bomber Command until July 1943 when he was replaced by General Frederick L. Anderson.

The Eighth Air Force began its bombing activity cautiously, starting in July 1942 with modest attacks with small groups of bombers on the coastal regions of occupied Europe; Generals Spaatz and Eaker were primarily interested in testing flight and bombing techniques and the validity of the basic theory of high-altitude daylight attacks against specific targets.

On August 17, 1942, a group of B-17s led personally by General Eaker successfully bombed the railway area of Rouen, and in the following months a certain optimism spread among the officers of the Eighth Air Force; it seemed that the American strategy was applicable successfully and with limited losses, General Eaker presented a detailed plan in four phases of systematic daytime bombing of Germany.

Beginning in October 1942, in fact, General Eaker received new directives that practically suspended the execution of his plans and the programs for expanding the bombing forces of the Eighth Air Force. The imminence of Operation Torch required the transfer of a part of the units to the new Twelfth Air Force just formed to provide air cover for the landings in North Africa; furthermore the main targets of the Eighth Air Force temporarily became the U-boat bases and the submarine shipyards.

Starting from 21 October 1942 the bombers of the VIII Bomber Command hit with reasonable results and limited losses, the bases of Lorient and Saint-Nazaire, while in the last months of the year and at the beginning of 1943 the French railway hubs of Lille and Romilly-sur-Seine were also attacked with some success.

General Eaker remained confident; in his opinion these actions demonstrated the validity of the tactics of the American bombers who apparently were able to hit with greater precision, suffering less losses than half compared to the British and inflicting, thanks to the defensive firepower of the heavy bombers organized in combat boxes, heavy losses on the German fighters.

VIII Bomber Command

VIII Bomber Command was a USAAF unit during World War II, formally active from 1942 to 1944. Together with VIII Fighter Command, it was part of the Eighth Air Force, the main air component of the United States deployed to bases in the United Kingdom to participate in the war in Europe.
Its main task was the strategic bombing of French, Belgian, Dutch territory occupied by Nazi Germany and above all of the territory of the Third Reich itself.
According to the strategic theories of American generals, VIII Bomber Command, equipped with an increasing number of excellent four-engine heavy bombers, launched continuous daytime air attacks theoretically against enemy military and industrial targets, flying in compact formations (combat boxes) at high altitude mainly without fighter escort, relying on the ability of its bombers to defend themselves with the fire of their numerous heavy machine guns.
At the cost of heavy losses, the bombers of VIII Bomber Command, led by capable and aggressive officers such as Generals Ira Eaker, Curtis LeMay, Haywood S. Hansell, constantly increased their power and effectiveness.
On February 22, 1944, the Allied High Command reorganized the command structure; the headquarters of the Eighth Air Force was used to form the centralized command of the United States Strategic Command in Europe, while the VIII Bomber Command assumed the new name of Eighth Air Force, which it maintained until the end of the war. After the entry of the United States into the war due to the Japanese attack on Pearl Harbor on December 7, 1941, in early January 1942 the heads of the Roosevelt administration decided that the United States Army Air Force should form an air force to be sent to Europe alongside the British Royal Air Force.
This unit was the Eighth Air Force (8th AF), which included the VIII Fighter Command and, precisely, the VIII Bomber Command, the latter officially born on 19 January 1942 in the USA and activated on 1 February at Langley Air Force Base.

About ten days later the unit joined the Eighth Air Force at Hunter Army Airfield in Savannah. The strategic planning of the American high command was extremely ambitious and envisaged a large and rapid increase in the forces available to the Eighth Air Force that would be accompanied by a massive logistical effort with the use of existing structures and the construction of almost a hundred new installations and airfields. The original plans foresaw that by August 1942 the Eighth Air Force would have 1,000 aircraft, which was to rise to 3,500 in April 1943; the detailed plans planned the initial constitution of 66 air groups, the VIII Bomber Command would have 700 four-engined heavy bombers at its disposal.

The organic structure of the USAAF included:

- At the base the Squadron, composed of 13 aircraft in the case of bomber units or from 23 to 28 if the unit was composed of fighter aircraft.
- 2-5 Squadrons formed a Group.
- 2 or 4 Groups then went to form the maximum tactical unit, that is the Wing.

A first detachment of bombers touched down in England on 23 February, but the bulk of the airmen arrived, without aircraft, starting from May 1942, after General Carl Spaatz, commander of the 8th AF, had agreed with the British all the administrative and logistical aspects. The headquarters was established at the RAF airport of Daws Hill, near High Wycombe (Buckinghamshire) and remained there until the end of the war; Brigadier General Ira C.

Eaker was instead put in charge of VIII Bomber Command, who, together with his superior Spaatz, was skeptical of the air warfare strategies employed by the RAF Bomber Command in the previous years. The two Americans, in fact, argued the uselessness and ineffectiveness of carpet bombing conducted at night, as the RAF did, while having maximum faith in precision bombing during the day, theoretically possible for American bombers thanks to the sophisticated Norden aiming system installed on their B-17E Flying Fortresses; furthermore, these planes were theoretically able to repel attacks from German fighters thanks to the powerful defensive armament available.

The first B-17E arrived at Prestwick (Scotland) on 1 July 1942, followed by 49 other aircraft of the same type by the end of the month. On 27 July, the first unit of the Eighth Air Force, the 97th Bombardment Group, became operational at Grafton Underwood (Northamptonshire), and within a short time four bomber wings were formed. General Henry H. Arnold, Commander in Chief of the USAAF, issued to these formations a priority order of targets to be hit in northern France: port and naval installations as well as war industries; aircraft and munitions factories; communications routes. The baptism of fire for VIII Bomber Command came on 17 August 1942 when the 97th Bombardment Group received the order to destroy the Rouen-Sotteville railway. General Eaker himself took part in the mission, commanding 12 Flying Fortresses protected by Spitfires supplied by the RAF.

- The 18 tons of bombs dropped did not touch the railway at all but there were no losses.

Two days later, on August 19, the same day as the failed raid on Dieppe, another 24 B-17Es, again escorted by the RAF, dropped some bombs around the Abbeville airport and over the Wehrmacht positions.

On September 6, during two simultaneous raids on the Saint-Omer-en-Chaussée airport and the aircraft factories at Méaulte, the first losses of the VIII Bomber Command occurred, with two bombers not returning. By the end of September the first Liberator Group entered the scene and on October 9, the VIII Bomber Command carried out its major raid, using 91 Flying Fortresses and 24 Liberators, against the armaments industries of Lille.

The final outcome, however, was disappointing: the bombers broke up their formations, five were shot down, and the factories were undamaged.

At the end of October, some aircraft were transferred to the newly formed Twelfth Air Force to provide air support for Operation Torch in North Africa, and on 5 December Spaatz went to head the Northwest African Air Forces, leaving command of the Eighth Air Force to Eaker, while General Newton Longfellow became commander of VIII Bomber

Command. From 17 August onwards, VIII Bomber Command had sent 957 bombers on missions, 780 of which had dropped 1,586 tons of ordnance..

A B-17 Flying Fortress crew of VIII Bomber Command saluted by Colonel Curtis LeMay.

In the second half of 1942, VIII Bomber Command, in parallel with its logistical and numerical reinforcement, radically modified its flight formations and bombing techniques to adapt them to the difficult mission of successfully completing long missions in the heart of enemy territory, by day and without fighter escort, searching for and hitting mainly industrial and military targets.

On the initiative of Colonel Curtis LeMay, the "Combat Box" tactic was born and adopted; LeMay believed that it was essential to obtain the best results that the bombers be deployed in formations of 18 or 21 aircraft divided into groups of three, carefully positioned at different altitudes so as to be able to organize a powerful and almost impenetrable fire screen in all directions with the 10-12 heavy machine guns that equipped each B-17.

Furthermore, LeMay ordered his men to fly in a straight line always at the same altitude, with a constant speed over the target, without wasting time with stragglers or damaged aircraft, without making evasive maneuvers and without worrying about anti-aircraft fire; in this way the formation would maintain cohesion, the danger of the defenses would be less and aiming with the Norden would be easier.

The combat box tactic, numerically reinforced to include even 54 or 108 aircraft, was from that moment the distinctive feature of the United States bombing air forces, guaranteeing increasingly effective results and allowing the bombers to reach and hit their targets in the vast majority of cases.

Colonel LeMay put his tactics into practice on November 23, 1942, personally leading the combat boxes of the 305th Bomb Group in the lead bomber against the French port of Saint-Nazaire; the raid was a brilliant success, the planes flew straight at high altitude over the target without suffering losses and hitting with precision.

In response to the Casablanca Conference, the commander of the Eighth Air Force, General Eaker, asked his superiors to reinforce the front line by sending in large quantities of bombers, he requested 944 by 1 July 1943 and 1,192 by 1 October, with which he felt sure he would reduce U-boat production by 89%, ball bearings by 76%, bombers by 65% and fighters by 43%, but his request was never granted: in October only 850 bombers would be active. Activity at the beginning of 1943 was reduced for the VIII Bomber Command.

On 27 January the first attack was carried out against a German target, the port and submarine shelters of Wilhelmshaven, but little damage was caused. Between January and February, small missions were then carried out on Saint-Nazaire, Lorient and Brest.

The activity intensified from March to the end of June with flights mainly directed always over France. Some of these ended with a success for the Americans, such as the one carried out on 18 March by 97 B-17s and B-24s over Bremen-Vegesack where seven submarines sank compared to only two bombers lost, but overall the bad weather, the FlaK and the German fighters, despite the use of the P-47 Thunderbolt as an escort fighter, however with insufficient autonomy, thwarted the efforts of the American pilots who suffered higher losses than their colleagues of Bomber Command without equaling their destructive power; between 1 January and 30 June 1943 the percentage of aircraft shot down was 6.6% and those damaged was 35.5%, while only 12.7% of the pilots of VIII Bomber Command hit their bombs within a radius of 274 meters from the target. The debut of the Martin B-26 Marauder was tragic, as on May 14 they dropped bombs on the power plant at IJmuiden (North Holland) with such a delayed-action bomb that the Germans managed to defuse them; when they returned to the same place three days later, the Luftwaffe's Messerschmitt Bf 109s destroyed 11 out of 12 of them.

In July, despite consistently high losses (6.8% of aircraft lost and 62.5% damaged at the end of the month), the VIII Bomber Command, now under the command of General Frederick L. Anderson, managed to score some victories, although it remained in the shadow of the RAF and the bombings that the Mediterranean Air Command was carrying out in Italy at that time.

On July 4, successful raids were carried out at La Pallice, Le Mans and Nantes, ten days later the activity of SNCAN at Vélizy-Villacoublay was interrupted for almost a month, and towards the end of the month the Fieseler and Heinkel factories, in Kassel and Seebad Warnemünde respectively, received severe blows which slowed down production considerably.

On 17 August 1943, exactly one year after its inception, VIII Bomber Command suffered a partial defeat in the famous Schweinfurt-Regensburg raid, which made General Eaker and his superiors realise that the bombers, without a long-range fighter to protect them all the way, were too exposed to Luftwaffe pilots.

The targets were the Messerschmitt factories at Regensburg and the ball-bearing factories at Schweinfurt, and the timing of the mission was designed to ensure that the force heading for the latter town would not encounter German fighters, forced to refuel after attacking the bombers over Regensburg.

The P-47 Thunderbolts watched over 146 B-17s led by Colonel Curtis LeMay heading for Regensburg to the Belgian-German border, then the Bf 109s and Fw 190s shot down 14 Flying Fortresses, while the others, after dropping their bombs on the target, diverted southwest towards Algeria, although another 10 aircraft were killed by German fighters from Austria.

At this point, another 230 B-17s were supposed to take off, commanded by General Robert B. Williams, and were to attack Schweinfurt, but the persistent bad weather over England slowed their departure, so that Hermann Göring's men had time to refuel and return to patrol the skies, causing 36 bombers to crash.

Of the 376 aircraft that had departed, the VIII Bomber Command did not see 60 return, even though on the other hand Messerschmitt had suffered considerable damage as well as the three Schweinfurt industries targeted by the offensive, among the first to experience a drop in productivity that, over time, the Americans would cause with their attacks on many other plants.

However, just two days later, on 19 August, the USAAF pilots took to the air again, although not to head for Germany, where they returned only on 27 September to carry out a Bomber Command-style carpet bombing of Emden, but for various French locations, also with the support, between 8 and 9 September, of the RAF, from which among other things the H2X radar was derived. All the missions were not demanding; on average a few dozen aircraft participated per raid, but they had the effect of further training the crews.

The negative trend in terms of losses, however, was confirmed again in October.

On the 8th of the month, in fact, 30 bombers failed to return from a raid on the Weser factories in Bremen-Vegesack and the following day the same fate befell 28 B-17s that fell over Marienburg and Anklam; at Marienburg, however, an exceptional precision bombing raid was carried out against the Focke-Wulf factories.

Eaker, not discouraged by the losses of crews suffered over Schweinfurt on 17 August, ordered a further bombing of the factories in the Bavarian city on 14 October.

The mission, judged by the RAF to be madness, involved 291 B-17s adequately escorted by 103 P-47s, but when these were forced to return to base to refuel, the German fighters, although hindered by the machine guns of the B-17s that shot down no less than 25, destroyed 60 Flying Fortresses irreparably damaging another 17, thus branding the day as "Black Thursday" for the American pilots who fell into a state of despair.

Arthur Harris, head of Bomber Command, invited Eaker to stop day flights in favor of night flights, but the American general refused.

For the rest of October, a single primary mission was carried out on the Gilze en Rijen airport, carried out not by chance on a day of bad weather to avoid losses, from which Eaker wanted to keep away also using, for the first time, the window countermeasure. In October, 9.1% of the aircraft used were lost and 45.6% were damaged.

After the defeat of October 14, VIII Bomber Command did not penetrate deeper into German territory and losses, in the last two months of 1943, stood at 3.7 and 3.4% of the aircraft sent on missions, respectively. The Wehrmacht's homeland was heavily overflown by heavy bombers, while France, Belgium and Holland were the preserve of B-26 Marauders.

In all these attacks, mediocre damage was inflicted on the pre-established targets, but the civilian and residential areas, despite Eaker's boast of conducting precision bombing, were nevertheless hit hard.

The first important missions of January 1944 were the bombing of the aircraft industries of Halberstadt, Oschersleben, Braunschweig and Magdeburg, attacked on the 11th of the month by 720 bombers protected by a large number of Anglo-American fighters, even if only the new North American P-51 Mustangs had enough autonomy to fly to the targets; because of this decrease in "surveillance", 59 bombers fell but 663 still managed to drop their bombs.

On January 29, 806 bombers effectively hit the aircraft industries of Frankfurt am Main and Friedrichshafen, this time with few losses, 12 aircraft to be exact. General Arnold, head of the USAAF, after receiving orders from Washington and SHAEF, reprogrammed the targets of the Eighth Air Force, of which VIII Bomber Command was a part, so as to deal with the German aircraft industry and everything connected to it: assembly plants, repair shops, airfields and ball bearing factories, as a priority in February 1944.

The first raids in this direction began on 3 February on Wilhelmshaven, continuing on the 4th on Frankfurt, on the 10th on Braunschweig and Gilze en Rijen, on the 11th again on Frankfurt.

A pause of about ten days followed, necessary to prepare for Operation Argument, the great Anglo-American offensive directed against the seventeen major aircraft factories and the twenty main airfields of Hitler.

On the morning of 20 February, the Eighth Air Force mobilised almost all its aircraft to strike factories on the Braunschweig-Magdeburg-Leipzig route and other areas (Tutow, Bernburg, Gotha, Oschersleben, Poznań, Berlin and Dresden). The following day the bombers returned to Braunschweig, Bernburg and Hallenstadt. On 22 and 23 February the missions were reduced to make way for the Fifteenth Air Force operating from Italy, but on the 24th the flights resumed on Schweinfurt, which suffered no significant damage, Gotha, Tutow, Kreising and Poznań.

On the last day of Operation Argument, February 25, about 2,000 aircraft from the Eighth and Fifteenth Air Forces of the USAAF headed toward Germany: the only target attacked by both large military units were the Messerschmitt factories in Regensburg, which were badly damaged, while the Eighth Air Force alone achieved success over the factories of Fürth, of lesser scope in the areas of Augsburg, Stuttgart, Diepholz and Rostock.

The history of the VIII Bomber Command was however over, in name but not in fact, already by February 22, 1944, when the USAAF was completely reorganized: General Ira C. Eaker was transferred to the supreme command of the Mediterranean Allied Air Forces, the Eighth Air Force became the United States Strategic Air Forces in Europe under the orders of General Carl Spaatz, and the VIII Bomber Command changed its name to Eighth Air Force, whose command was placed under General Jimmy Doolittle.

Combat Box

The Combat Box was the tactical combat formation used by United States Army Air Force strategic heavy bombers during World War II. The combat box was also known as the "staggered formation". The advantages of this formation were:
- From a defensive point of view, the ability to provide a great deal of firepower with the bombers' heavy machine guns.
- From an offensive point of view, the ability to drop the war load in a short time and concentrated on the target.

This formation was initially designed to follow the pre-war doctrine of the United States Army Air Corps which envisaged that heavy bombers deployed in concentrated formations could attack and destroy targets by day and without fighter escort, relying on the curtain of fire provided by the numerous Browning M2 heavy machine guns with which they were equipped.
Furthermore, the USAAF bomber tactic of flying at high altitude required the use of a concentrated bomb release system and therefore the combat box continued to be used for its offensive effectiveness even after the arrival of efficient escort fighters which, flying well ahead of the combat boxes on air superiority missions against German fighters, greatly reduced the threat from enemy air defenses.
The design of the combat box has been credited to Colonel Curtis LeMay, commander of the 305th Bombardment Group in England in 1942-1943; in reality the Eighth Air Force had been experimenting with different tactical formations since the time of its first bombing mission in Europe, on 17 August 1942, some of which were already known as boxes. LeMay's group created the "Javelin Down" combat box in December 1942 and this formation became the basis for the combat box variants that were used later.

The custom of calling a concentrated formation of aircraft a "box" comes from the diagram images from above, in profile and from the front, which appear to place each individual bomber in an invisible box-shaped area..

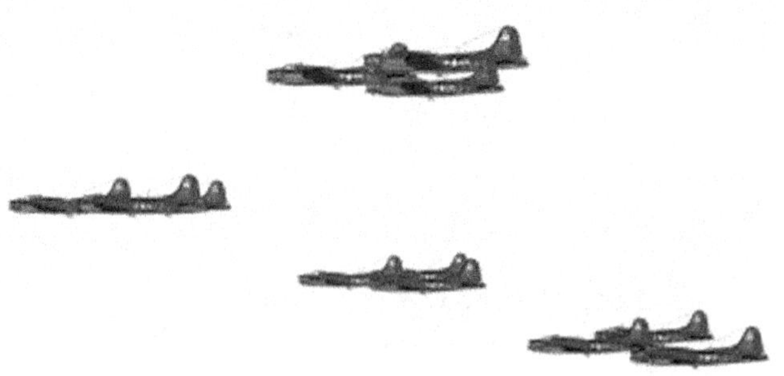

Colonel LeMay was an extremely energetic and combative officer, absolutely determined to continue with the utmost determination the strategic bombing missions; he believed it was essential to adopt a formation that would guarantee the achievement of the objective and the precision of the bombing; furthermore the flight deployment would have to allow to limit the losses and repel the attacks of the German fighters demonstrating the validity of the general USAAF strategy of daytime bombing at high altitude without fighter escort.

LeMay gave precise instructions to his men: the bombing formation would have to be maintained at all costs and the planes would have to fly at high altitude straight on the objective, absolutely avoiding, even if attacked by fighters and targeted by anti-aircraft fire, evasive maneuvers that would have dispersed the formation.

Flying straight at high altitude and at high speed the bombers would have reduced the travel time in the danger zone reaching the objective sooner, which would also be hit with precision thanks to the Norden aiming system. Finally, LeMay's "Javelin Down" deployment would have maximized the bombers' considerable defensive capabilities, as they could organize a belt of fire with their many powerful heavy machine guns.

To overcome the doubts of his subordinates and galvanize his men, LeMay threatened court-martial for crews who failed to execute their mission by breaking formation, but he also stated that he would personally fly the lead bomber and lead the planes to the target..

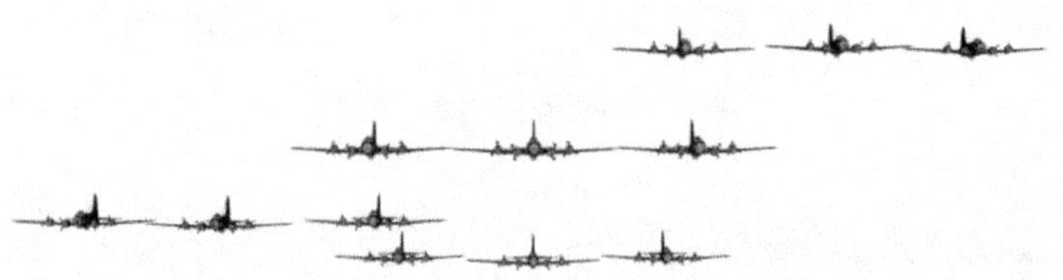

LeMay's combat box scheme was as follows:
- Three squadrons, each consisting of 6-7 bombers, flew diagonally at different altitudes in the direction of the sun.
- The three squadrons, called High element, the highest, Lead element, the middle one, and Low element, the lowest one, were each formed by two patrols of three bombers each arranged in the classic V formation.

In the V formation, the central plane was the Leader while the one on the right was the Deputy Leader, "vice-commander". The formation was staggered and the second V of the Low element was diagonally aligned with the second V of the High element flying higher. LeMay's group flew in this arrangement and each combat box of 18 aircraft was spaced about 2.5 kilometers from the others.

The next combat box followed about 30 meters below the altitude of the Lead element, while the others flew to the left or right of the Lead element based on the position of the sun.

LeMay put his tactics into practice on November 23, 1942, by personally flying the 305th Bomb Group's combat boxes in the lead bomber against the French port of Saint-Nazaire; the raid was a brilliant success; the planes flew straight and high over the target without losses and struck accurately.

By the end of 1942, the "Javelin Down" formation of 18 to 21 planes was being used by all the groups in the Eighth Air Force.

The combat box formation devised by LeMay was designed to include all the planes in a bombing group, but as the months of 1943 passed, the numerical strength of the Eighth Air Force continued to grow and American officers began to employ larger variants of the combat box to fit three entire bomber groups into a single compact formation.

Thus the "Combat Wing" was formed with 54 planes; three groups of 18 aircraft each gathered together in a combat box, always based on the triangular formula with a bomber or group of bombers leader in the center and two other bombers (or groups) in a V formation, one at a higher altitude and one lower, close together to ensure mutual defense.

In the new variant the groups were arranged horizontally and flew at a higher altitude to reduce vulnerability to attacks by enemy aircraft.

The wing box with 54 aircraft was further modified over time to better counter the new tactics of the German fighters who from mid-1943 began to regularly practice the method of attacking bombers head-on.

An attempt was made to make the formation even more compact; furthermore, since at the end of May only four groups of B-17s were available in the Eighth Air Force, composite groups were formed by squadrons from different groups; on some occasions a fourth group was added to the wing box which thus took on a diamond shape.

The fourth wing box group, however, flying at the rear of the formation, often proved vulnerable to the Luftwaffe's tactics of attacking bombers flying at the outer points of the formation first. The wing box was generally spread over 900 metres vertically, 2.1 kilometres deep and 600 metres horizontally and proved an effective formation but difficult to maintain in action; the subsequent combat wings generally flew 9.5 kilometres apart.

Overall, the combat wing could engage an impressive number of defensive weapons, forming a formidable barrage against German fighter attacks; the 54 bombers had a total of 648 12.7 mm heavy machine guns which could each fire up to 14 shells per second at a range of 550 metres.

To cope with frontal attacks by German fighters, the bombers also received in June 1943 a new front turret equipped with two more heavy machine guns which further increased the defensive firepower of the combat box.

Despite its power and cohesion, the wing box formation had some weaknesses; a major disadvantage was that the lower and upper elements, flying at either end of the formation, were more vulnerable and had less protection; there was also a risk of an aircraft being hit by bombs dropped by higher-flying bombers if it lost its position in the box. In the summer of 1943, the Eighth Air Force dramatically increased its strength to 16 B-17 and 4 B-24 groups, and by June 1944 it had 39 groups in active service; regular organizational charts were updated, and heavy bomber groups increased in strength from 35 to 62 aircraft, thanks to the huge influx of new bombers from the fall of 1943; the use of composite groups was abolished, and many groups began flying two boxes at once on the same mission.

The 54-aircraft wing box used by Eighth Air Force B-17s required experience, skill, and discipline from the crews to maintain proper formation; turbulence in the flight of the lead bombers could add to the difficulty of maintaining position within the various boxes.

The 54-aircraft formation was designed primarily to provide great defensive firepower at a time when the primary threat to the bombers was from Luftwaffe fighters, but by May 1944, the German anti-aircraft gunnery weapon became the most dangerous weapon to Eighth Air Force aircraft; under these conditions, the high command decided to revert to the combat box with 36 aircraft deployed in a looser formation.

This arrangement was used regularly in the latter part of the war, except when heavy air opposition from German fighters was expected.

In October 1943 the radar-guided Pathfinder group entered into action for the first time, deemed necessary to improve the results of the bombing in adverse weather conditions of the combat boxes with 36 aircraft.

In addition, to minimize the risk of collision, it was decided to double the elements of three aircraft in each squadron from two to four and to station all three bombers at the same altitude.

Colonel LeMay, who had been transferred to command the 3rd Bomb Division, immediately introduced the new combat box with twelve aircraft in a diamond formation, believing it to be superior to other tactics; therefore, when he was promoted to brigadier general in August 1944 and transferred to the Pacific and Southeast Asia front to take command of the Twentieth Air Force in India with the task of launching Operation Matterhorn, he adopted this formation for his Boeing B-29 Superfortress ultra-heavy strategic bombers.

A variant was also studied with a formation with four squadrons of nine aircraft each in a diamond formation, to improve the concentration of bomb releases. In this formation each wing box followed in the wake of the previous one and the deployment was also easier to escort and protect.

The close positioning of the four squadrons, however, was difficult to maintain and increased the risk of a bomber flying lower down being hit by bombs dropped by bombers higher up. In special situations the 36-aircraft box would forgo the lowest squadron to reduce these risks. Combat boxes with 36 or 27 bombers were used universally in 1944, although a diamond formation with four squadrons of ten aircraft each was developed for the B-24s of the Eighth Air Force and Fifteenth Air Force.

During the winter of 1944-45, reducing bomber losses to FlaK became a priority. The 27-aircraft combat box became the basic formation for the B-17s throughout 1945, spaced widely apart laterally to avoid catastrophic damage to the entire formation in

the event of a single enemy hit. In addition, the wing bombers flew further forward than the leader elements, creating a box that was 230 meters (750 ft) vertically, 200 meters (650 ft) deep, and 360 meters (1,100 ft) laterally.
This final version of the combat box allowed for excellent payload release modes, was easy to control and maintain, and reduced the target for German anti-aircraft fire.

The Bombing of Schweinfurt

Like glistening silver insects, with white contrails trailing behind them, the Flying Fortresses flew in a 10-mile long formation, leaving the cliffs of the English coast behind them. It was August 17, 1943, exactly one year to the day since the American Eighth Air Force began bombing Hitler's 'Festung Europa', Fortress Europe, from bases in Britain.

The weather at the American bases in East Anglia was foggy and overcast, and the Flying Fortress crews had been anxiously waiting to hear whether the missions would go ahead or not; some had to wait as long as six hours.

The tension was compounded by the importance that everyone, from the commander in chief down, assigned to that day's mission: it was the first completely strategic bombing operation, destined to annihilate a vital part of German industry and, consequently, to shorten the duration of the war. "Now, boys," an officer said in one of the preliminary reports, "we're in for a tough one today.

We're going to hit some ball bearing factories in a town in Bavaria called Schweinfurt.

The route we'll take will take us over the center of Germany, both ways. Those factories produce about half of Germany's ball bearings, and if we destroy them, our raid will be a success, even if only a few..."

The rest of the sentence was drowned out by a chorus of groans. These men had heard the story of the 'suicide mission' many times before, and they knew it wasn't all just talk.

"The altitude will be 23,000 feet, and we'll try to split the defense. The 3rd Division will go in first and hit Regensburg (the second largest aircraft factory in the Reich) nearby, then continue on to North Africa. The other two air divisions will hit Schweinfurt and return to England. Let's hope the plan works, because if we don't fool them, we risk having 300 to 400 fighters on us." Prophetic words.

The plan didn't work and more than 500 young Americans lost their lives on that mission.

The entire plan was based on perfect synchronization, 146 Flying Fortresses, with nearly 200 fighters escorting them for the first hour, were to leave the English coast at Lowestoft, zigzag over the North Sea towards Holland, then turn south towards Belgium, then south-east in Germany to Mannheim, and then straight east to attack the Messerschmitt factories in Regensburg.

A fine target, but, in reality, it was mostly a diversionary maneuver to divert the attention of the German interceptors. Ten minutes after the lead formation took off under the command of Curtis LeMay, 230 more B-17s and escort fighters under Brigadier Robert Williams were to take to the skies for the ball bearing factories at Schweinfurt. To further confuse the situation, a mixed formation of British Typhoons and American Mitchell medium bombers was to simultaneously launch a raid over the Strait of Dover and lure as many German fighters as possible southward, toward Brittany.

H-hour was set for 8:30.

At that time, however, fog was covering eastern England like a soggy blanket. LeMay's groups, based near the Norfolk coast, were the first to notice a change. Shortly after 9:00, they began to glimpse the end of the runway, although the ceiling was still zero. By 9:30 they were all up and making a wide circle, the diameter of which was the distance from Norwich to the Wash, killing time while the rest of the Eighth Air Force came up to join them.

If they had left more than 10 minutes of interval with another formation, the whole mission would have been a waste of time..

A longer interval, in fact, instead of causing confusion, would have turned into a warning to all the fighter control centers of Germany. Every minute that passed saw the plan gradually fall apart. Today, in hindsight, it is easy to argue that the entire operation should have been canceled immediately and rescheduled for another day.

But who can say what was going through the mind of Brigadier General Frederick L. Anderson, sitting in his command bunker in High Wycombe, solely responsible, not knowing what to do? Pressure was coming from all sides to deliver a mortal blow to the German strategic industry.

Pressure was coming from within the American Air Force to prove that the strategy of mass raids was the right one.

Meteorologists argued that, even if for the moment it was under clear skies, central Europe would then be covered in clouds for at least a fortnight.

For a whole hour the formation destined for Regensburg remained in the holding pattern, watched attentively, every movement of every aircraft, by radar operators from all the bases in Holland and Northern Germany, and they too began a vain solitary dance, just as a boxer fights a ghost in his corner before the gong for the first round.

The Typhoons and Mitchells took off as usual and flew their futile provocative mission over the Pas-de-Calais, and Anderson still hesitated.

At 10.00 he had to make up his mind. If the Regensburg formation was to land on the unknown airfields of North Africa with a little light left, it had to get going.

The teleprinters went off in all the control towers on the East Anglian plain, and the 3rd Division of the Eighth Air Force turned east and away. The fog was beginning to lift further south and inland, where the groups destined for Schweinfurt were based, and little by little they too took off.

Delays piled up as group after group entered the circuit; then, at 1.15pm, they turned south, over the Suffolk coast, across the North Sea and beyond the bounds of reason into a different world. Most of the second wave crews did not see a single fighter escort once they cleared the Dutch coast. RAF Spitfires were already aloft to greet them, but the long-endurance Thunderbolts took off 9 minutes later than planned and never reached them.

It is said that General Anderson reasoned that if a 10-minute delay might cause confusion in the ranks of the Luftwaffe, a 3-hour delay would do the same.

But to ignore the capabilities of the German radar network in this way is nothing short of criminal.

While a 10-minute interval between the two attack formations would have forced the fighter controllers to divide their forces, the long delay allowed them to direct all available aircraft, fully fueled and fully loaded, against the two formations, one at a time. "By the time the fog had cleared enough for us to take off," recalls one of the survivors of the Schweinfurt mission, "the 34th Division must have already bombed Regensburg and must have been on its way to Africa. Instead of helping us by dividing the fighters, they had simply warned German Fighter Command that this was a major operation.

"We emerged from the fog at about 300 meters and, once we had reached 7,000 meters, headed for the Continent. A layer of thick clouds that extended from 5,000 to perhaps 8,000 meters blocked our path and we could not squeeze through in formation and hope to hold it. Colonel Gross, who commanded the 1st Air Division, had a difficult decision to make: go over and risk having the objective also covered by clouds, go for a secondary objective, or go under the blanket.

The advantage of going up to 7,000 meters was that you would be high enough to make things difficult for the fighters, whether Messerschmitts or Focke-Wulfs. Whereas at lower altitudes, between 4,500 and 5,500 meters, they were in their element."

And it was at that altitude that Colonel Gross decided to send his entire bombing formation down. And it was the finishing touch, the final nail, hammered into an already overfilled coffin. The massacre began immediately.

Gross's formation, which paid for its commander's mistake, lost 10 four-engined planes in as many minutes. The Americans, with 11 12.7 mm machine guns per plane, were heavily armed and flew in tight protective formation.

When, at the end of the day, it was announced that 288 enemy fighters had been shot down, it was probably an exaggeration; but the fighters really did what they wanted. We know that 147 Fortresses were lost, 60 never returned, 27 had suffered such damage that, even though they returned, they were discarded as unusable, 60 arrived in North Africa in such a condition that they could not even be repaired. They too were left aside and, in the end, dismantled for use as spare parts. Not that the first wave fared much better.

A pilot who belonged to the last formation, obviously the most vulnerable, recounts: "Our four-engine aircraft was almost constantly in danger from the debris that was flying towards us. Emergency hatches, normal doors, parachutes opened too early, human bodies and assorted fragments of Flying Fortresses and German aircraft were flying at us in the wake of the formation.

We continued to fly in that wake of a desperate air battle, in which it was normal to see four-engine aircraft and fighters disintegrate in the air". At 10.17 near Woensdrecht,

I saw the first few thin, imprecise flak clouds bloom in the sky near us. A few minutes later, two FW-190s came at us, heading 1 o'clock, at our altitude, and shot through the formation that preceded us in a frontal attack, damaging two Fortresses on the wings and disengaging under us in a half-roll. Both four-engined planes that had been hit began to emit smoke trails, but held their ground. As the fighters flew past us at a very high speed, our Group's machine guns opened fire.

The pungent smell of burning powder filled the cockpit and the B-17 shook completely, under the recoil of the nose and turret machine guns. Before it disappeared from our sight, I noticed fragments breaking off from the wing of one of the fighters. It was a taste of battle. The crew sniffed the air. of trouble.

There was something desperate in the way those two fighters had come at us immediately, right out of the climb, without any preliminaries.

For a few seconds the intercom was full of advice: 'Lead them more'…'short bursts'…'don't waste ammo'…'more coming in a minute'.

Three minutes later, the gunners reported fighters climbing in from all sides, singles and in pairs, both FW-190s and Me-109s. Every machine gun on every B-17 in our Group was up, filling the sky with a net of tracers.

Casualties on both sides, two Fortresses from the lower group and one from the Group ahead of us broke away in flames from the formation with their crews parachuting; several fighters went down in flames, their pilots swinging down on dirty yellow parachutes.

I noticed that there was an Me-110 lurking out of range on our right; remained with us all the way to the target, apparently to signal our position to groups of interceptors waiting ahead. At the sight of all those fighters, I had the distinct feeling of being trapped.

Our Group's survival prospects suddenly seemed very low, as the fighters seemed to be skipping over other formations to get at us. In a wide 180-degree turn that showed off their yellow 'noses', a formation of 12 Me-109s came straight at us, spreading out to 2 o'clock, in pairs and fours at a time, and began the dance. Something silvery spun in the air over our starboard wing. I recognized it: it was one of the main boarding doors.

A few seconds later, a dark object came tumbling through the formation, narrowly avoiding several propellers. It was a man, crouched with his knees close to his head, looking like a diver in a triple somersault.

I didn't see his parachute open.

A B-17 slowly broke away from the formation to the right, maintaining altitude. In a fraction of a second, the four-engine plane disappeared with an explosion that left only four small fireballs in the sky, the fuel tanks, which quickly burned up in the fall.

I saw two fighters explode, not far below us, and disappear in a yellow blaze; four-engined planes losing altitude in every condition of damage, from burning engines to torn-off tailplanes; friendly and enemy parachutes descending and, against the green backdrop of the ground, numerous funeral pyres of fallen planes, showing the way. A hallucinatory scene.

I watched a B-17 slowly bank to the right with its cabin on fire. The co-pilot climbed out of his window, holding on with one hand, picked up his parachute, hooked it on, let go and went straight into the horizontal stabilizer. I think the impact electrocuted him. His parachute did not open.

Ten minutes, twenty minutes, thirty minutes, and no pause in the attacks. The fighters lined up like people queuing for bread, and came at us. Every second marked by time contained a grenade. Our B-17 was still vibrating from the recoil of its machine guns, and the air inside was thick with smoke.

It was cold in the cabin, but when I turned to look at the pilot, I noticed that the sweat from his forehead was running down his oxygen mask. He handed me the controls for a while.

And it was a blessing to concentrate on holding our position in formation instead of watching those endless fighters bearing down on us. It was possible to forget about them.

Then the two barrels of the upper turret machine guns began to hammer away at a foot from my skull, providing a realistic imitation of shells exploding in the cockpit.

A B-17 from the squadron ahead of us, its extra fuel tanks (Tokio tanks) on the tip of its right wing on fire, slowed until it was about two hundred feet above our right wing.

Seven men managed to get out by parachute: four jumped from the bomb bay, waiting a few seconds before opening their parachutes: one jumped out of the nose, opened his parachute too soon and almost got caught in the tailplane; another jumped out of the port side machine gun hatch, delaying the opening for a few seconds.

The tail gunner jumped out of his hatch, apparently pulling the opening cord before he was completely out: the parachute opened suddenly, missing the tailplane by a hair's breadth and giving him such a jolt that it took off both his shoes; he remained hanging, inert, from his harness, while the others, after their parachutes opened, immediately showed signs of life.

Then the B-17 began to lose altitude in a medium flat spin and I did not see the pilots jump.

I saw him for the last time several hundred meters below us, with his starboard wing completely engulfed in yellowish flames. After a full hour of continuous attack, it seemed certain that our Group would be wiped out. Seven of our men had been shot down, the sky was still full of fighters, and it was only 11:20 (35 minutes to the target).

I doubt if any of us had really thought about going much further. I had already mentally accepted the fact that I would die; it was just a matter of when that would happen. I learned firsthand that a man can resign himself to certain death without giving in to panic.

Our Group's firepower had been reduced by 33%; ammunition was running low.

The tail machine guns had to be resupplied from another position. The gunners were starting to get tired.

At the IP (the starting point of the straight bombing path) at 1150, an hour and a half after the first of a series of at least 200 individual fighter attacks, the pressure eased, even though enemy aircraft were still nearby. We turned onto the IP at 1154 with 14 B-17s still in the formation; two of them, badly damaged, fell behind soon after they had dropped, then headed for Switzerland.

Weather conditions at the target, as during the entire flight, were ideal. Flak was negligible. The formation dropped immediately after the commander. As we turned, heading for the Alps, I was eerily gratified to see a rectangular column of smoke rising from the target. The rest of the mission saw a marked change of scene. A few fighters made a few passes over us toward the Alps.

A small town on the Brenner Pass sent up a few in vain flak hits. We circled Lake Garda, just long enough to give stragglers a chance to get back into formation, then continued slowly toward the Mediterranean. The prospect of having to make a crash landing for lack of fuel as we approached Africa, and the sight of more B-17s going into the sea, seemed like nothing after the crazy nightmare of the long flight across southern Germany.

At 1815, with all the red reserve lights on, the seven Fortresses still in formation turned into the landing pattern of a base in North Africa. Our crew was unharmed.

The damage to the Fortresses was slight: a few holes in the tail from flak and 20 mm rounds. We slept on the hard ground, under the wing of our four-engined plane.

But the good earth seemed softer than a silk pillow."

(Source: History of Aviation).

The Aphrodite Project

Project Aphrodite and Project Anvil were the code names used by the USAAF and USN (United States Navy) during World War II to bomb enemy bunkers and hardened enemy structures using B-17s, especially the B-17F, and PB4Y-2s converted into smart bombs, such as those targeted in Operation Crossbow.

The plan called for B-17s, which had been decommissioned, nicknamed "robots", "babies" or "drones", armed with high-capacity explosives, and piloted by radio control to strike German fortifications such as U-boat bunkers and V-weapons (retaliatory weapons) sites.

It was hoped that this project could match the British success with the Tallboy and Grand Slam free-fall bombs, but it proved dangerous, expensive and unsuccessful.

Of the 14 missions flown, none resulted in the destruction of a target; many aircraft lost control and crashed or were shot down by flak, and many pilots were killed. However, a small number of aircraft did come close to their intended targets.

One notable death was that of pilot Joseph Patrick Kennedy Jr., the older brother of U.S. President John F. Kennedy.

The program officially ended on January 27, 1945, when General Carl Andrew Spaatz sent an urgent message to Jimmy Doolittle: "Aphrodite is not to be launched against the enemy until further orders."

In late 1943, General Henry H. Arnold had directed electrical engineers under Brigadier General Grandison Gardner at Eglin Field, Florida, to equip some of the bombers, already retired from the war, with automatic pilots so that they could be controlled remotely.

The plan was first proposed to Major General James H. Doolittle in early 1944: Doolittle approved the plan on 26 June for Operation Aphrodite, and assigned the 3rd Air Division to prepare the drone, which was to be designated BQ-7.

In the US Navy's similar project, Operation Anvil, the drone was designated BQ-8.

The final assignment of responsibility was given to the 562nd Squadron at RAF Honington in Suffolk. Similarly, on 6 July 1944 the US Navy's Special Attack Unit (SAU-1) was formed under ComAirLant, with Commander James A. Smith as the officer in charge, for immediate transfer to command Fleet Air Wing 7 in Europe to attack V-1 and V-2 sites with PB4Y-1s converted to attack drones.

The older Boeing B-17 Flying Fortress bombers were stripped of all their standard combat armament and all other non-essential equipment (armor, guns, bomb racks, transceiver, seats), reducing the aircraft's weight by about 12,000 pounds (5,400 kg).

The aircraft's canopy was removed to facilitate the pilot and co-pilot's ejection by parachute; AZON remote control radio equipment was added, along with two cockpit-mounted cameras to provide a view of both the ground and the main instrument panel, for transmission to an accompanying CQ-17 "mother" aircraft.

The drone was loaded with explosives weighing twice as much as a normal B-17 bomb load. The British Torpex explosive used for the purpose (8,100 to 9,070 kg loaded on board with an impact fuse) was itself 50% more powerful than ordinary TNT.

A relatively remote location in Norfolk, RAF Fersfield, was designated as the base of operations.

RAF Woodbridge was initially considered because of its longer runway, but the possibility that a damaged aircraft diverted to Woodbridge might collide with a loaded drone caused concern.

A B-17F used during Project Aphrodite and used against the "Fortress of Mimoyecques"; the aircraft crashed shortly before the target due to a control error; pilot Lt. Fain Pool and engineer Sgt. Philip Enterline nevertheless managed to successfully parachute out.

The remote control system was insufficient for safe takeoff; each drone had to be flown by a volunteer pilot and flight engineer to an altitude of 600 meters before handing over control to the operators of the CQ-17 "mother" drones.

After verifying the drone's remote control, the two-man crew would arm the explosive payload and then eject from the cockpit.

The CQ-17 "mother" would then direct the transformed drone aircraft to the target. By the time the training program was complete, the 562nd Squadron had ten drones and four "mothers."

Major missions included:

- Watten - August 6, 1944 - two B-17 bombers, aircraft 30342 and 31394, experienced control problems and crashed into the sea. B-17 30342 impacted Gravelines, probably due to FlaK damage, while B-17 31394 crashed into the sea after several circles over the important industrial and port town of Ipswich. All crews abandoned their aircraft in time.
- Heide - August 1944 - four drones; three failed to reach their target due to control malfunctions, while the fourth crashed but was close enough to the target to cause significant damage and high casualties.
- Mission 549/Le Havre - 13 August 1944 - The B-17 drone with 907 kg of bombs missed its target and a de Havilland DH.98 Mosquito was also destroyed by exploding bombs.
- Heligoland U-boat Bunker - 11 September 1944 - B-17 30180, hit by enemy flak, crashed into the sea.
- Heligoland U-boat Bunker - 15 October 1944 - both drones, B-17 30039 Liberty Belle and B-17 37743, missed their target due to bad weather.
- Herford Marshaling Yard - 5 December 1944 - B-17 39824 and B-17 30353 failed to identify their target due to cloud cover, so both were diverted to bomb Haldorf, but both crashed outside the town.

Post-war use

After World War II, the B-17 was deemed obsolete and the United States retired most of its aircraft. Crews moved the bombers across the Atlantic to the United States, where most were scrapped.
Following the formation of the United States Air Force in 1947, the remaining B-17s (designated F-9s and later RB-17s) entered service with the Strategic Air Command (SAC) from 1946 to 1951.
A few were used by the Air Rescue Service for deep-sea search and rescue operations in the late 1940s through the mid-1950s.
By the late 1950s, the last B-17s in service had become QB-17 target drones, DB-17P drone controllers, and VB-17s.
The last operational mission was flown on 6 August 1959, when DB-17P 44-83684 directed QB-17G 44-83717 out of Holloman Air Force Base, New Mexico, as a target for an AIM-4 Falcon air-to-air missile fired by an F-101 Voodoo.
A retirement ceremony was held a few days later, after which the last aircraft, 44-83684, was retired from service. During the final year of the war and the immediate postwar period, the US Navy acquired 48 B-17s for patrol and recovery operations.
Since most Flying Fortresses were built by Douglas or Lockheed rather than Boeing, a more logical type designation would have been the P4D-1W or P3V-1G.
Twenty-four B-17Gs (including one B-17F upgraded to the G version) were operated by the Navy as PB-1Ws; the "W" signified antisubmarine duty.
They were equipped with a large radome, designed for an AN/APS-20 search radar, mounted under the fuselage, and additional internal fuel tanks were added to increase range. They were also repainted in dark blue, a standard livery employed by the Navy in late 1944.
Most of the aircraft were built by Douglas and flew from the Long Beach factory to the Naval Aircraft Modification Unit in Pennsylvania during the summer of 1945, where they were fitted with radar.

However, the war ended before the PB-1Ws could be used, so the installation of defensive armament was canceled.

The first PB-1Ws were assigned to Patrol Bomber Squadron 101 (VPB-101) in April 1946. The aircraft eventually evolved into early warning aircraft, using their APS-20 radar.

In 1947, PB-1Ws were employed in units with both the Atlantic and Pacific fleets. VPB-101 on the East Coast were assigned to Test and Evaluation Squadron FOUR (VX-4) and assigned to Quonset Point Naval Air Station, Rhode Island. Later in 1952, VX-4 became Early Warning Squadron TWO (VW-2) and moved to Patuxent River, Maryland. The secondary mission was antisubmarine defense and hurricane reconnaissance.

The first early warning squadron was formed in 1952 with four PB-1Ws, based at Harbers Point Air Force Base in Hawaii. Two B-17s were assigned to the Navy as XPB-1 for various development programs. The first was transferred to the Navy in June 1945 and the second in August of the following year.

The latter was used by the Cornell Aeronautical Laboratory in a test program for the development of jet engines.

Boeing XB-38 Flying Fortress

The Boeing XB-38 Flying Fortress was a four-engine strategic bomber built by the American company Boeing in the 1940s that remained at the prototype stage.

- Derived directly from the B-17 Flying Fortress, it differed from its predecessor mainly for the adoption of a different type of engines, four 12-cylinder V-shaped liquid-cooled instead of the radials adopted by the original project.

In 1942, a collaboration was undertaken between Boeing and the Vega Aircraft Company, a subsidiary of the Lockheed Corporation, aimed at creating a variant of the Boeing B-17 Flying Fortress bomber with better performance and that could make up for the possible lack of availability of the Wright R-1820 radial engines, originally adopted, in the series production of the same.

The XB-38 was the result of this project, created with the aim of evaluating the possibility of equipping the B-17 with the Allison V-1710, a liquid-cooled V-12 equipped with turbocharging.
Starting from a Flying Fortress airframe, the modifications took less than a year to complete and the prototype flew for the first time on May 19, 1943.

- The XB-38 proved capable of reaching a slightly higher speed than the B-17, but after only a couple of flights it was forced to ground due to problems with the engine exhaust systems.

Once the problem was solved, the tests continued for another eight flights, until June 16 of the same year when, during the last flight, the number 3 engine, the inner one on the right wing, suffered malfunctions and caught fire, forcing the crew to bail out.
The example was destroyed and the development program was cancelled also due to the need to use the V-1710 engines on fighter aircraft projects including the P-38 Lightning, P-39 Airacobra, P-40 Warhawk, P-51A Mustang and P-63 Kingcobra..

Allison V-1710 Engine

The Allison V-1710 was a twelve-cylinder V aircraft engine built by the American Allison Engine Company and used on USAAF aircraft during World War II.
The V-1710 is the only engine of this type designed and produced in the USA during the conflict to be used in combat. Its debut was not the best due to some inconveniences related to the supercharging system but later, thanks to subsequent developments, it became a powerful and reliable engine.
The Allison Engine Company, a company belonging to the General Motors group, began designing a liquid-cooled engine in 1929 in response to a request from the U.S. Army for an engine of about 1,000 hp (750 kW) to be used on new bombers and fighters.
- To facilitate its production and installation, the engine had to be able to be equipped with different reduction groups and a turbocharger. In this way, engines that could be mounted on any aircraft could come off the same production line.

The Great Depression slowed development and it was not until December 14, 1936 that the engine was flown for the first time mounted on a Consolitated XA-11A. On April 23, 1937, the V-1710-C6 passed the 150-hour test required by the U.S. Army.
- The power output, 1,000 hp, was in line with the request and the Allison engine was one of the first series aircraft engines to reach it.

The V-1710 benefited from General Motors' construction philosophy based on the versatility of installation of the different components.
The engine could be considered to be made up of two parts.
- The central part was the actual engine.
- On this standard central core, the various accessories, rear part, and reduction groups, front part, could then be mounted, thus satisfying the different needs of all aircraft.

Furthermore, this type of approach made it very simple to replace both the supercharging system and to modify the compression ratio, allowing the creation of a range of engines that could be effective from 2,400 meters up to 7,900 meters.

Another feature of the V-1710 was the ability to rotate the propeller both counterclockwise and clockwise quite easily.

- During construction, a special crankshaft, a set of supercharging gears, a set of accessories and a starting system appropriate for the direction of rotation chosen were fitted.

The V-1710 has often been criticised for the lack of a mechanical supercharger for high altitudes.
Usually, this criticism is made by comparing the latest versions of the Merlin produced under license in the United States as the Packard V-1650, equipped with a two-stage supercharger. The engine, however, was designed, following the requests of the U.S. Army, with only a single-stage turbocharger and if better performance at higher altitudes had been required, a new type of turbine could have been fitted.
The first V-1710s had a maximum combat altitude limited to 5,000 metres, but being available in large quantities they were

widely used especially in the North African theatre of operations.

Technical Features

- Engine type: 60° V
- Number of cylinders: 12
- Fuel system: Bendix Stromberg carburetor with automatic fuel regulator
- Displacement: 28.03 L (1,710.6 in³)
- Bore: 139.7 mm (5.5 in)
- Stroke: 152.4 mm (6.0 in)
- Distribution: SOHC 4 valves per cylinder. Sodium-insert exhaust valves
- Fuel: 100 octane gasoline
- Cooling: Pressurized liquid: 70% water and 30% ethylene glycol
- Supercharger: Single-stage centrifugal
- Power: 1,325 hp (988 kW) @ 3,000 rpm
- Specific power: 0.77 hp/in³ (35.3 kW/L)
- Length: 2,502 mm (98.53 in)
- Width: 744 mm (29.28 in)
- Height: 1,046 mm (41.18 in)
- Compression ratios: 6.65:1
- Empty weight: 655 kg (1,445 lb)

Boeing YB-40 Flying Fortress

The Boeing YB-40 Flying Fortress was a four-engine aircraft obtained by modifying the American B-17 Flying Fortress bomber, converting it into a heavily armed aircraft to be used as an escort for other bombers during the latter part of World War II.

At the time of its development, long-range fighters such as the North American P-51 Mustang had not yet entered production in large quantities and were therefore not available to escort bombing missions all the way from England to Germany and back. In the early 1940s, during World War II, the USAAF 8th Air Force stationed in England took part in the strategic bombing of German cities carried out by the Allied air forces.

The long ranges necessary to reach targets deep in Axis territory were compatible with the typical autonomy of heavy bombers of the time, but not with that of the fighters that were supposed to escort the formations. It was therefore necessary to design long-range fighters specifically for this role, but while waiting for the completion of the various development phases, an alternative solution was also considered that could be relatively simple, quick to implement and that would solve the problem, while waiting for the availability of new aircraft.

In 1942, the USAAF authorized the design of heavily armed and armored versions of the bombers already in service.

A collaboration was undertaken between Boeing and the Vega Aircraft Company, a subsidiary of the Lockheed Corporation, aimed at producing a heavily armed variant based on the Boeing B-17 Flying Fortress bomber, equipped with enough firepower to constitute a serious threat to enemy fighters.

The construction of the prototype, designated Project V-139, was authorized in the same year and construction began in September, converting the second example of a B-17F (B-17F-1-BO), serial number 41-24341, which Vega Aircraft produced under license.

Shortly thereafter, on November 10, the model, which received the official designation XB-40, was flown for the first time, confirming the project's feasibility in a short time.

The first order for the supply of 13 examples had actually already been issued in October, and a second one followed for another 12 examples made in January 1943, entrusting the transformations to Douglas Aircraft at its factories in Tulsa, Oklahoma.

The XB-40 prototype built by Lockheed Vega (Project V-139) through the conversion of the second B-17F produced, the B-17F-1-BO (S/N 41-24341).

The first production example was completed at the end of March 1943. A supply of 20 examples was ordered for operational service tests, company designation Vega Project V-140, designated by USAAF conventions YB-40 in the escort role and TB-40 in the training role. Since Vega had priorities in the production of other projects, the assembly work of the YB-40/TB-40 was transferred to Douglas.

The task of the YB-40 was to provide a massive fire cover to defend against German fighter attacks during bombing missions, both in the approach phase to the target and in the return phase to the base in England.

During actual operational use, however, a serious tactical problem was encountered as the YB-40s were unable to match the performance of the B-17 Flying Fortresses they escorted, both when they were loaded with bombs and, even more so, when they had dropped their war load.

Of the 13 examples assigned to operations in Europe, and which constituted the initial order, one was damaged due to a forced landing on the Isle of Lewis while on a transfer flight from the United States of America and the remaining 12 were assigned to the 92nd Bomb Group (H) based in England, later redesignated 327th Bomb Squadron.

Between 29 May and 16 August 1943, the YB-40 participated in 14 of the 19 combat missions planned by the Eighth Air Force, although on the mission of 26 June all assigned YB-40s failed to enter formation with the bombers and were forced to return to base.

Of the 59 planned, data referring to the total of the overall presence of the aircraft in the 13 missions carried out, in the 48 participations in the missions the YB-40s were credited with 5 certain kills plus two probables against only one YB-40 shot down, hit by the FlaK of the German anti-aircraft on 22 June and fallen at Hüls.

In the last 5 raids the mission tactics were modified, modifying the attack formation with the simultaneous use of two YB-40s positioned in the lead to better protect the commander. Despite the failure of the project in the assigned operational role, the YB-40 introduced some important changes that would be integrated directly into the production of the last substantial development of the B-17, the B-17G:

- The introduction of the Bendix Turret (the Chin turret), also adopted in the last production version, the B-17F.
- Offset waist station.
- The improved tail gunner station, commonly known by the nickname "Cheyenne" after the work done at the Cheyenne modification center.

The aircraft was visually differentiated from a standard B-17 by the adoption of a second dorsal turret positioned where the bomber version had installed the radio compartment, that is, just aft of the bomb bay and before the ventral Sperry bubble turret.

The single 12.7 mm Browning M2 machine guns, originally adopted for each defensive position, were replaced by a twin system, similar to that present in the tail, again based on two coupled M2s. In addition, the aiming equipment was replaced with a Bendix turret, also equipped with two 12.7 × 99 mm Browning machine guns, positioned under the nose of the aircraft.

The existing side-mounted machine guns, positioned on both sides of the fuselage at the height of the bomb bay and initially removed from the configuration, were reinstated in England, bringing the planned quantity back to 16 machine guns and using the bomb bay as a magazine for ammunition.
Protective plates were also positioned to protect the gunners' positions.
The aircraft was found to have a full load weight of about 4,000 pounds (about 1,800 kg) more than that of a fully equipped B-17, which translated into greater difficulty in reaching cruising altitude.
  • A B-17F reached 6,096 meters in 25 minutes, while to reach the same altitude, a YB-40 needed 48 minutes, almost double.

The lower performance was due in part to the greater weight of the equipment and in part to the greater aerodynamic drag due to the additional defense positions.
YB-40s flew the following operational missions:

- 22 June 1943

Attack on the IG Farben synthetic rubber plant of the Industrie Chemische Werke in Hüls.
The plant, which accounted for a large percentage of Germany's synthetic rubber production capacity, was severely damaged. Eleven YB-40s participated in the raid; aircraft number 42-5735 was lost, having been damaged by flak and then shot down by a Focke-Wulf Fw 190 A-2.

The 10 crew survived and were taken prisoner.

- 25 June 1943

Attack on Blohm & Voss in Oldenburg. This was the secondary target, the primary target of Hamburg being obscured by clouds. Seven YB-40s participated in this raid with two German aircraft claimed down.

- June 26, 1943

Attack on the Luftwaffe depot at Villacoublay, France (primary target) and the Luftwaffe airfield at Poissy, France.
The five YB-40s assigned to the attack were unable to form a squadron and returned to base.

- June 28, 1943

Attack on the U-boat base at Saint-Nazaire. The base's only entrance was destroyed in the raid. Six YB-40s took part in this attack and one German aircraft was claimed destroyed.

- July 4, 1943

Attacks on aircraft factories at Nantes and Le Mans, France. In these raids, two YB-40s were sent to Nantes and one to Le Mans.

- • July 10, 1943

Five YB-40s participate in the attack on Caen/Carpiquet airport.

- • July 17, 1943

Two YB-40s sent on a raid against Hannover, then recalled due to bad weather.

- • July 28, 1943

Two YB-40s sent to attack the Fieseler aircraft factory in Kassel.

- • July 29, 1943

Two YB-40s participate in the attack on the U-boat yards in Kiel.

General characteristics

- Crew: 10
- Length: 22.60 meters
- Wingspan: 31.40 meters
- Height: 5.80 meters
- Wing area: 141.90 m2
- Empty weight: 24,900 kg
- Loaded weight: 28,800 kg
- Max. take-off weight: 33,565 kg
- Engine: 4 Wright R-1820-65 radials with turbocharger
- Power: 1,200 hp (895 kW) each
- Maximum speed: 470 km/h
- Cruising speed: 315 km/h
- Range: 3,640 km
- Service ceiling: 8,900 meters
- Wing loading: 231 kg / m²
- Armament: 18 Browning M2 machine guns, 12.7 mm caliber. Typically 14 or 16 were used, although space was available to house 30. Total rounds available: 10,700.

The surviving B-17s

To date, only 39 surviving B-17s remain in the United States; of these, 12 aircraft are still airworthy, two B-17F models and ten B-17G models. Several are well-known names, including "Memphis Belle," "Sentimental Journey," "Nine O Nine," and "Aluminum Overcast."
An additional 18 B-17s are on display in the United States, including "Virgin's Delight" in Atwater, California, and "Shoo Shoo Shoo Baby" at the U.S. Air Force Museum in Dayton, Ohio.
Finally, 9 aircraft are undergoing restoration or are in storage.

- B-17G - 44-83514 - Sentimental Journey - Mesa, Arizona - airworthy.
- B-17G - 44-85828 - I'll Be Around - Tucson Air and Space Museum - on static display.
- B-17G - 44-83546 - Memphis Belle - Military Aircraft Restoration Corp of Ahaneim - airworthy.
- B-17G - 43-38635 - Virgin's Delight - Castle Air Museum of Atywater - on static display.
- B-17E - 41-2446 - Swamp Ghost - Planes of Fame Museum of Chino - on static display.
- B-17G - 44-83684 - Piccadilly Lilly II - Planes of Fame of Chino - undergoing refurbishment for Air Worthiness.
- B-17G - 44-6393 - Starduster - March Field Air Museum of Moreno Valley - on static display.
- B-17G - 44-85778 - Miss Angela - Palm Springs Air Museum - airworthy.
- B-17G - 44-83563 - Fuddy Duddy - Martin Aviation, Inc. of Santa Ana - airworthy.
- B-17G - 44-85738 - Preston's Pride - AMVETS at Mefford Field, Tulare - on static display.
- B-17G - 44-83624 - Sleepy Time Gal - Air Mobility Command Museum at Dover - on static display.

- B-17G - 44-83863 - Unnamed - Air Force Museum at Eglin - on static display.
- B-17G - 44-83542 - Piccadilly Princess - Fantasy of Flight Museum at Polk City - on static display.
- B-17G - 44-83525 - Suzy Q Fantasy - Flight Museum at Polk City - in storage.
- B-17G - 44-83790 - Unnamed - Don Brook of Douglas - undergoing restoration.
- B-17G - 44-83814 - City of Savannah, Mighty Eighth Air Museum - on static display.
- B-17E - 41-2595 - Desert Rat - Michael W. Kellner - undergoing restoration.
- B-17G - 44-83690 - Miss Liberty Belle - Grisson Air Museum - on static display.
- B-17G - 44-83884 - Miss Liberty - Global Power Museum at Barksdale - on static display.
- B-17E - 41-9032 - My Gal Sal - National World War II Museum in New Orleans - on static display.
- B-17G - 44-83575 - Nine-O-Nine - Collings Foundation - airworthy.
- B-17G - 44-85829 - Yankee Lady - Yankee Air Force, Belleville - capable of air navigation.
- B-17G - 44-83559 - Bee Strategic - Ashland Air & Space Museum - on static display.
- B-17F - 42-3374 - Homesick Angelo - Offutt Air Force Base, Omaha - on static display.
- B-17D - 40-3097 - Swoose - Dayton Air Force National Museum - undergoing restoration.
- B-17G - 42-32076 - Shoo Shoo Shoo Baby - Dayton Air Force National Museum - on static display.
- B-17F - 41-24485 - Memphis Belle - Dayton Air Force National Museum - undergoing restoration.
- B-17G - 44-85813 - Unnamed - Champaign Aviation Museum, Grimes - undergoing refurbishment.
- B-17G - 44-83785 - Evergreen - International Evergreen Aviation & Space Museum McMinnville - airworthy.
- B-17G - 44-85790 - Lacey Lady - Milwaukie Bomber Foundation - on static display.

- B-17G - 44-85599 - Reluctant Dragon - Dyess Air Force Base, Abilene - on static display.
- B-17G - 44-85718 - Thunderbird - Lone Star Flight Museum, Galveston - airworthy.
- B-17G- 44-83872 - Texas Raiders - CAF Gulf Coast, Houston - airworthy.
- B-17G - 44-83512 - Heavens Above - Lackland Air Force Base, San Antonio - on static display.
- B-17G - 44-83663 - Short Bier - Aerospace Museum Hill AFB, Ogden - on static display.
- B-17F - 44-8543 - Chuckie - Training Services, Inc., Virginia Beach - airworthy.
- B-17G - 44-85740 - Aluminum Covered - Experimental Aircraft Assoc., Oshkosh - airworthy.
- B-17F - 42-29782 - Boeing Bee - Museum of Flight, Seattle - airworthy.
- B-17E - 41-9210 - Unnamed - Wulcan Warbirds Inc., Seattle - undergoing restoration

Boeing C-108 Flying Fortress

The Boeing C-108 Flying Fortress was a four-engined aircraft obtained by modifying the American B-17 Flying Fortress bomber, converting it into a transport aircraft and used operationally by the United States Army Air Forces (USAAF) during the latter part of World War II.

During the war, many B-17s were retired from the front line due to wear and tear and, of these, four were converted to the role of transports, even though the circular section fuselage was not well suited to contain the cargo compartment.

- The first C-108 (designated XC-108) was built on the basis of a B-17 suitably modified for VIP transport; in fact, the armaments and armor were removed.

The entire fuselage was modified with the addition of an office, extra portholes and a kitchenette. Between August 1943 and March 1944, another B-17 was converted into a cargo aircraft (designated XC-10A). In the hope of converting the obsolete B-17s from bombers to cargo aircraft, a specialized conversion shop was set up at Wright-Patterson Air Force Base.

For the cargo version, the bulkheads were removed and the opening in the fuselage for dropping bombs was sealed.

Versions

- XC-108, a version with 38 seats and side windows used as a personal transport for General Douglas MacArthur.
- XC-108A, equipped with a large side cargo door.
- YC-108, for transporting executives.
- XC-108B, for transporting fuel.

As can be seen from the acronyms, in which Xs designate experimental aircraft and Ys pre-production models, none of these actually entered production.

www.ingramcontent.com/pod-product-compliance
Lightning Source LLC
LaVergne TN
LVHW050610200726
843508LV00010B/1793